Bottle Collecting

finding, collecting and displaying antique bottles

Bottle Collecting

finding, collecting and displaying antique bottles

by

Edward Fletcher

London

Blandford Press

First published 1972

by Blandford Press Ltd,
167 High Holborn, London WC1V 6PH

© 1972 Edward Fletcher

ISBN 0 7137 0608 2

Text set in 12 on 13 Bembo and
printed in Great Britain by
Unwin Brothers Limited
Woking and London

List of Contents

To John Webb, Michael Beach, Ron Rowland, Johnnie Condon, John Whittle, Joan Allen, Eric Foster, Alan Biddlecombe, and all treasure hunters, amateur and professional. May Lady Luck sit firmly on their shoulders as Long John Silver's parrot sat on his.

Acknowledgements

The author and publishers are grateful to the following who have helped to produce this book:

John Wood, who did the line drawings;

Miss Betsy Almond, who supplied Fig. 10;

The *Illustrated London News*, who supplied Fig. 22.

The remainder of the photographs were supplied by the author.

There has been in recent years a great surge of interest in all things old and beautiful. The collecting bug has bitten and we have become a nation of bric-à-brac lovers. Record prices are asked and paid for every collector's item imaginable and those who can afford to buy form an endless queue. The rest of us look on with a little sadness and a little envy as the horse brasses, antique weapons, porcelain dolls, coins, medals, floral chamber pots and copper kettles are carried off to other people's display cabinets. We go home empty handed or console ourselves with plastic imitations.

Against this background of sky-high prices it comes as no surprise to find that more and more frustrated collectors are turning their backs on the antique stalls. They have discovered a new way of owning old and beautiful objects; and they have become totally engrossed in a hobby which combines all the thrills of a treasure hunt with all the pleasure of building up a fine display of antiques. In short, they have become bottle collectors.

Old bottles are beautiful. The glass is flecked with air bubbles and tears; the stoneware burned to a fine gritty texture never seen on modern pottery. Colour varieties include aqua green, cobalt blue, ruby red, amethyst and milky white—all in endless shades; and because each bottle was hand-made in a wooden mould by a craftsman who loved his work, each is a work of art. Bottle lips and the glazes on stoneware were hand-applied and their crudeness and individuality makes every bottle a unique collector's piece. Indeed, there are so many variations in colour, maker, shape, type and embossing that most collectors concentrate on one particular class of bottles. They may collect only quack medicine bottles embossed with amusing Victorian advertising; they may specialize in beer bottles or glass marble mineral waters; or they may prefer the simple beauty of early, sheared-lip syrup bottles. But whatever their preference they will never exhaust the varieties which abound in every class.

And where are these beauties to be found? The fact is that they are all around us—in rivers, in ponds and in

7

long-forgotten rubbish dumps. Equip yourself with a digging fork, a glass-bottomed bucket and a probe rod and you can join in the great adventure of finding your own antiques and involve yourself in the fascinating detective work of site-hunting. You will study the history of your home town or village with a renewed interest: gathering information at the public library, gleaning clues from old town hall records, researching the sites of demolished pubs and rediscovering long-lost village ponds. When you embark on your first dig the whole family will want to join in. Children love bottle-hunting and wives and girl friends are enchanted by long-necked cobalt blues and ruby red perfumes. And after your first dig you can look forward to all the fun and pleasure of cleaning, identifying and displaying your own antique bottles. Indeed, a totally absorbing hobby.

This is the first book to be written on collecting British bottles and I have written it with the beginner in mind. It includes chapters on every aspect of bottle collecting and explains in detail the methods used to locate sites, dig bottles and identify and date your finds. Advice on cleaning and displaying bottles is included and I have also written something of the history and chemistry of bottle manufacture. For readers who wish to sell their finds, a chapter on setting up a stall at a weekend antique market and a guide to pricing has been added. Newcomers will find all they need to know in the following pages, and I hope that experienced collectors will take pleasure from reading in one volume all they have taught themselves about the hobby over the years. It is to these 'bottle buffs' I dedicate this volume. Their knowledge has made possible the birth of a new hobby; their experience will surely help it grow. To Ruth Hurst Vose, Assistant Curator at The Pilkington Glass Museum, St. Helens, to Roy Morgan of Kollectorama, Wellingborough, and to other members of The British Bottle Collectors' Club I say a very special 'thank you' for all their help.

Many schools, clubs and other organizations are turning to bottle collecting as an excellent group activity. For teachers, youth leaders and club organizers I have added a brief chapter which I hope they will find useful when planning a bottle dig or organizing their own club. Such projects provide an excellent means of combining outdoor adventure with research and display activities.

As other finds, apart from bottles often turn up on a dig, I have included a brief chapter on clay tobacco pipes and pot lids and given instructions on how these can be repaired for display.

Finally, a note to overseas readers. Millions of 19th-century bottles were exported from Britain as food and drink containers and as ships' ballast. Dig any 19th-century dump in North America or Australia and you will almost certainly find British bottles of that period. Similarly, French, Dutch and German bottles are not uncommon in British dumps; and all overseas readers are likely to find some of the bottles illustrated in this book on the sites they search. The evolution of bottle shape and the methods of bottle manufacture followed an almost identical sequence in Britain, North America and Europe between 1800 and 1900 with a few notable exceptions; and the disposal methods for unwanted bottles were universal. It follows that almost all of the advice given in this book on finding, identifying, cleaning and displaying old bottles will apply throughout the world.

Fig. 1 Admiring the re-
sults of a dig on a late
19th-century dump

If your first glimpse of Victorian bottles is a fine display in a collector's home, you will find it difficult to believe that the collector actually dug them out of the ground or pulled them from the mud of a riverbed or stream. It is hard to credit that the bottles were buried for a hundred years or more. The glass shines with air bubbles and fluorescence; the stoneware is polished to a satin sheen; the colours and shapes are so varied it seems unthinkable that such beautiful objects were actually thrown away. Yet millions of these containers are to be found discarded throughout the country.

1 Finding bottle sites

Although the population in the 1800s was far less than it is today, there were many more bottles in the average family's weekly throw-outs. The majority of foods and beverages were purchased in glass or stone containers, plastics were unheard of, and packaging in cardboard cartons was a newfangled idea frowned upon by the buying public. Dry tea was sold in bottles, toothpaste was brought in stone jars, chemists bottled their own patent medicines, young girls bought their cosmetics in milk-white pots with pretty lids, old men spent fortunes on hair restorers in superbly embossed flasks and canned beers were fifty years away. Boot polish, ink, fruit, tobacco, scouring powder, confectionery and almost every household item except fresh meat, fish and vegetables was sold in a bottle or jar. Most of the empties found their way into dumps, rivers and ponds; to find them you must first carry out some careful historical detective work.

The key to all successful bottle hunting is research, and the best place to make a start is close to home. Where you live matters little. Excellent finds can be made both in crowded cities and on open stretches of moorland. If you live in the wilds of Cornwall there is no need to catch a train to London in the hope of finding better sites; and if you live in London there is no need to envy the countryman. Make up your mind now to concentrate on finding your bottles locally. Later, as you become a more experienced collector, you might travel fifty miles or more to dig a site which contains the bottles in which you chose to specialize;

but your early expeditions are more likely to be successful in home surrounds. However little interest you have taken in local history in the past, you are sure to know more about your own town or village than a place half a day's journey away. Remember, too, that you are a beginner and will probably aim at quantity rather than quality when collecting. Bottles are heavy, bulky and difficult to transport long distances without damage. That should help you avoid the temptation to travel in the hope of more productive sites. There are plenty of old bottles to be had within a few miles of your home. Let us make a start on the research that will lead you to them.

The public library should be first on your list of research **Libraries** centres. Visit it often and tell the librarians what you are looking for; they will be delighted to help you in your research. Borrow every local history you can lay your hands on, however dull the author's style; and ask the librarians for Victorian diaries by local writers, any old maps or photographs that are available, and any local records which are stored there. If you know the title or author of a book which you think might be of interest but which is not stocked, the library will probably be able to obtain a copy for you. A national lending service is operated which enables you to borrow books from other libraries on your local tickets. Make use of this service when researching sites in other towns.

You will have little success at the library if you simply flip through the index of a book to find R for rubbish dumps! I have not found such a reference in any local history book, but I have found many subtle clues which have led to first-class sites. Look instead for chapters dealing with 19th-century industries, with expansion and with the growth of population in the 1800s. And do take down careful notes of anything that interests you.

Large tracts of wasteland were reclaimed in Queen Victoria's reign for civic projects such as public parks and recreation grounds. It was an era of expansion when new homes and new factories appeared almost overnight and much of the land needed for this growth was reclaimed from former marshes. This was done by dumping household rubbish on low-lying, waterlogged sites which were unsuitable for agriculture. Many 19th-century factories, parks and recreation grounds occupy land which was once marshland and they rest on firm foundations of old and valuable bottles.

Maps of the district drawn before the factories and parks appeared will often show the land as being waterlogged, and if you find such clues you should note these sites as worthy of a thorough search. Many of the factories are now derelict and it is not usually difficult to obtain permission for a dig. Even the parks and recreation grounds, which will probably still be in use, can provide excellent bottle sites. They are almost always flanked by ponds and streams because of their former waterlogged condition, and a careful search along stream banks and pond sides will often reveal exposed layers of the old dump, while the streams and ponds are certain to hold valuable finds.

It is quite likely that there was a glassworks in your district a hundred years ago. They were not uncommon because of the huge demand for bottles, and even small towns could boast two or three bottle makers. Local histories often carry references to former industries and if you can pinpoint the site of a glassworks you could find an excellent bottle site. Mark it for particular attention even though the factory may have disappeared long ago. Thousands of rejected and out-of-date bottles were buried near old glassworks, and the dumps occasionally come to light during demolition or building work. The sites of old breweries are worth noting for the same reason.

Mining and quarrying are industries to look out for because they provided many dumping sites. When a mine, quarry or chalk pit was abandoned it was, and still is, common practice to use the workings as a refuse site. If you can find 19th-century workings you are guaranteed excellent bottles. Concentrate on the smaller sites because these are more likely to have been filled quickly and they will not have a top layer of modern rubbish. They are

shown on old maps as pits, quarries and mines.

You will often find references to lime kilns in Victorian local histories, particularly if the district has soil which requires lime as a fertilizer. Many old farms had lime kilns where chalk was burned to produce lime. These kilns were quite large, stone-built ovens, usually constructed close to roads so that cartloads of chalk could be drawn alongside. As they fell into disuse they made convenient dumps and some can still be found overrun by blackberry patches alongside modern roads. Excellent clues to their locations are found in field names which are often mentioned in local histories or marked on old maps. The name 'Furze Field' usually indicates a kiln nearby because furze, or gorse, was used as a fuel to burn the chalk.

Nineteenth-century editions of your local newspaper are excellent sources of information on old dumps and provide a remarkable insight into the everyday life of the community a hundred years ago. Most local newspapers date from Queen Victoria's reign or earlier and it is usually possible to visit their libraries for research purposes.

Unlike local history books, newspapers often give space to the subject of rubbish dumps. Unauthorized dumping made headlines in old newspapers just as it does today and you should look out for irate letters from local farmers whose pastures had just received an unlawful cartload of junk. Read all reports of local council meetings most carefully because the topics discussed by Victorian councillors are the very topics which interest today's bottle collectors—parks, recreation grounds, factory sites and rubbish dumps.

Old newspaper photographs should be studied carefully. Views of local landscapes can be particularly interesting when compared with the modern scenes they illustrate. Try to pick out valleys, slopes and depressions which have now disappeared. Levelling of sites by filling in hollows with rubbish was common practice during the last century.

Information about local industries, including glassworks and breweries, is often obtained by reading old newspaper articles and classified advertising columns; you must also look out for illustrated Victorian advertising. Quite often you will see advertisements showing bottles and jars which will turn up on your digs into local dumps. If the bottles are unembossed, such advertisements are invaluable aids to identification. They not only provide you with a picture of the bottle or jar, but they also reveal the original contents, the maker of the product, the original cost, sizes available, as well as the use, merits and virtues of whatever it was the bottle originally held. Search for these advertisements in other publications—parish and county magazines, almanacs, old trade catalogues and medical journals—and make careful notes on unknown bottles and jars you come across. They will prove extremely useful in future research.

Newspapers and magazines

If you live in a city or a large town, research at your municipal offices could prove rewarding. Organized refuse collection and disposal came earlier to towns and cities than to country districts and it is often possible to locate very early rubbish dumps by reading official records. Unfortunately many of the earliest and best dumps in cities and towns are now built over, but there are exceptions.

Coastal towns and seaports are worth investigating in this way, particularly if the local coastline has cliffs. Disposal of rubbish by tipping over sea cliffs was quite common in the 19th century as a means of preventing erosion. These dumps were rarely built on when completed and their exact locations can often be found in official records. Coastal salt marshes were reclaimed in a similar way, and many sea walls and Victorian harbour installations were constructed with the help of household refuse.

Towns whose populations have declined or remained static since the 19th century often have large old rubbish dumps which are still accessible because the sites have not been used for housing or industry. Modern population movements indicate the best areas for such towns; there are many in Scotland, some in Wales, and one or two in the north and west of England.

Even if you live in a booming and fast-expanding city or town where all the old dumps were built on long ago, your local town hall can still provide information which will lead you to excellent finds. Visit the Town Planning Department and ask to see the Planning Register. This is a list of applications made by both private citizens and companies to carry out construction work within the local council's administrative area. All councils are required by law to keep such a register which must always be available for public inspection. In it you will find details of plans to demolish houses, build roads, install water pipes and carry out the hundred and one activities and projects which are forever changing the fabric of cities and towns.

The Planning Register will tell you where a particular project is to take place, what the work involves, who is responsible for carrying out the scheme, and whether or not planning approval has been granted. If you read that a building contractor has received planning permission to demolish a Victorian mansion and erect in its place a multi-storey office block on a site which your earlier research pin-pointed as a dump, you could have a bonanza site on your hands.

Unrecorded dumps will often turn up during modern building and construction work. Use the Planning Register to make a list of all construction schemes due to start in the town within the next month, and visit as many locations as you can reach. Keep a sharp look out for bottles and broken glass in trench walls and mounds of earth moved by the builders. Try to make a friend of the bulldozer driver on the job; ask him to let you know if he unearths an old dump or turns up any old bottles. These men uncover and re-bury scores of old dumps every year and you should never miss an opportunity to talk to them about their work. Many, having seen beautiful old bottles and jars uncovered in this way, have become collectors themselves; and almost all will be able to show you a glass marble bottle recovered from the jaws of a trenching machine and kept as a souvenir.

Talking to old people

This is one of the most interesting methods of researching sites and one which can be used everywhere. Old people love to talk about the past, and listening to their reminiscences can lead to many excellent bottle finds. Perhaps you have a grandparent or other elderly relative whose help you can enlist in your hunt. Visit him or her, steer the conversation around to old bottles, and you could have the exact locations of several interesting dumps within half an hour!

Other readers will find that one of the best ways of getting in touch with knowledgeable old people is to enlist the help of the voluntary organizations which care for the aged, such as the W.V.S. Workers in these welfare services are in touch with most old people in the area and will often be able to suggest the very person you should talk to.

I have found it pays, when meeting these old folks for the first time, to take along a few samples of my bottles to show them what I am looking for. I produce a glass

marble bottle or a stone ginger beer and ask the old gentleman or lady if he or she remembers when such bottles were
in common use. Invariably they do remember and will
often go on to recall how, as children, they broke the glass
bottles to recover the marbles after drinking the last drop
of lemonade (see p. 50). It was a common enough children's
pastime until at least 1925; and it was one of the reasons why
this type of bottle went out of use. It was a dangerous
method of collecting marbles and also accounts for the fact
that there are relatively few unbroken specimens in old
dumps.

Approaching the subject of bottle sites in this oblique
manner is by far the best method when talking to old people.
It gives them time to recall their childhood memories;
it can often bring out other useful snippets of information;
and it provides many old people with something they
thoroughly enjoy—an hour or two of friendly conversation.

Of course, the human memory is frail. Every old person
you meet will not be able to recall exactly where his father
or grandfather dumped the family's rubbish; you may have
to talk to half a dozen old people before you get a cross-
reference on a site which is accessible today. But I guarantee
that your time will not be wasted.

Two interesting facts I have come up with after talking
to a great many old folks about bottles are worth noting.
Firstly, they are usually very informative about the uses to
which bottles were put sixty or seventy years ago. Many
an unembossed bottle of mine has been correctly identified
by someone who remembered buying such a bottle as a
child. Information about other sizes, what the product was
used for, the shops which sold it and what the original
label was like have all been revealed during these meetings.

Secondly—and this will be of use to you when you
become a specialist collector—I have found that old men
have better memories for beer bottles, whisky flasks and
other masculine products; whereas the ladies can always
be counted on to recall perfumes, household products and
medicinals.

One of the most appreciated ways of repaying old people

for their time and the useful information they can pass on is to offer them one or two of the old bottles you find on a site which they have suggested. Never has my offer of an old bottle, perhaps a local beer or a long-forgotten perfume, been turned down. Indeed, most have been given pride of place on a mantelshelf with family portraits and other valued possessions.

This method of research is always rewarding whether or not it leads to bottle sites; but it would be foolish to expect the immediate success that a friend of mine had recently when he talked to an old man about ginger beers. The old gentleman took him out to his garden shed and revealed row upon row of rare, two-tone ginger beers with transfer maker's marks. 'My brother collected this lot when he was a boy,' said the old man. 'You're welcome to them if you clear them all out. I need the space for my gardening tools.'

A rare stroke of good fortune indeed! But even without such luck you could soon be digging a site containing similar prizes following a chat with someone who spent a childhood surrounded by the very bottles we value so much today.

Rivers, streams, canals and ponds

There are probably as a many bottles underwater as there are bottles buried in the ground, and if you research the histories of local rivers, canals, streams and ponds you will find some first-class bottle-hunting sites.

If earlier investigations at libraries, newspaper offices and town halls indicated the sites of former glassworks and breweries along riverbanks you should find many old bottles in the water. Mark the sites as worth a visit after heavy rains and during drought periods, because at such times you can expect a rich harvest of finds. Flood water has enormous power and can scour the mud on a riverbed to a depth of several feet. Bottles disturbed in this way will be carried by the flood water to the first bend or meander on the river below the dumping site. Here, on the inside bend, the power of the current always slackens and heavier objects, including bottles, will be deposited in the sediment

Fig. 3 Ready for a river-side bottle hunt. This home-made rake is ideal for getting at bottles in deep water

which collects at such points.

During drought periods when the water level is low many old and valuable bottles and jars can be picked up along the riverbank. This is also an excellent time to examine the bed of the river closely in the hope of finding areas of broken glass, pottery and clay tobacco pipe fragments which might indicate the site of an unknown riverside dump not associated with a glassworks or brewery.

On tidal rivers a copy of the local tide tables will prove extremely useful. These tables are sold by local port and river authorities for a few pence per copy and you should always refer to them when planning visits to tidal sites. Time your visit so that you arrive at the riverside as the tide begins to ebb and you will be able to spend several hours on the riverbanks searching areas of mud and shingle newly uncovered by the falling tide.

There are many other fascinating bottle sites on rivers. Pubs are obvious examples as many riverside pubs have histories which span hundreds of years. Rare bottles including free-blown specimens dating from the 16th and 17th centuries have been found in rivers near waterside pubs and you should not neglect those in your area.

Bridges can be equally rewarding. I have not yet discovered what it is that makes drunken revellers throw empty bottles from bridges into rivers as they wind their merry ways homeward after a riotous evening at the local hostelry. Perhaps it is the delightful noise bottles make when they hit the water; or simply a convenient method of disposing of empties without digging holes. Whatever the reason it is certainly a universal practice which has continued for centuries. Every bridge on every river has a variety of

Fig. 4 Clues to a riverside dump: bottles, pottery and other objects clearly seen beneath top soil

bottles beneath its arches. The older the bridge the more likely are you to find really old bottles; and you should note every bridge in your area as worth at least one visit. The sites of fords, which pre-date bridges and can hold ever rarer finds, are even more important.

You may live in an area where the local river has a flood history. If this is so early dumps could turn up almost anywhere along the riverbanks. Many Victorian flood prevention schemes owe their success to an available supply of household rubbish with which the riverbanks were heightened and strengthened. One of the best methods of finding this type of dump in the absence of written evidence is to take a boat trip along the river and examine the banks carefully. Look for dark bands of soil containing pieces of broken glass and pottery and you may be on the site of a flood prevention dump.

Mooring and docking points on rivers make good sites on which to search for bottles in the water. Barges and other river craft have moored at these spots, usually chosen for ease of access or a good depth of water, for hundreds of years and many a prize bottle has gone over the side of a vessel hereabouts.

Docks and harbours large enough to take sea-going vessels should be earmarked as excellent search areas. Many foreign bottles can turn up beneath harbour walls; and it is sometimes possible to locate large quantities of bottles which were used as ships' ballast in the 19th century. They were dumped over the side before cargoes were loaded and they can be found today at low tides.

Canals and streams should be researched in a similar way. Canals are particularly interesting because they were important transport routes for only a few years and the majority of bottles and jars which lie on their muddy bottoms are early Victorian specimens. Look at most canals today and you will see only a tangle of weeds and rusted, derelict lock gates. It is perhaps difficult to recall that during their heyday they were the equivalent of our modern motorways. As many as one hundred barges would pass through a lock in a single day on the busier routes; and many thousands of men and women lived and worked along the network of man-made waterways which linked cities and towns in Queen Victoria's reign. Best spots for bottle finds are locks, canal-side pubs and the areas around the villages and hamlets where canal folk bought their food and drink.

Streams, although narrower, can hold large quantities of old bottles. They were often used as dumping grounds, especially in areas where there was no boat traffic and loss of depth by dumping was unimportant. They were also occasionally cleaned out by farmers who were more interested in their importance to local drainage systems. Old bottles and other household rubbish taken from them during cleaning were used to strengthen their sides and in country districts stream banks often hold many bottles. In towns the mud on the bed of the stream will hold better prospects.

Ponds of all descriptions should be looked at closely by bottle collectors. Village ponds, farm ponds, quarry ponds and fish ponds have all been used as dumps in the past. The best ponds of all, and the most difficult to find, are those which were completely filled with rubbish during previous centuries. A friend of mine found one recently and dug out fifty 18th-century, free-blown seal bottles. Lucky man! My best filled-in pond find to date was brimful with glass marble bottles. I managed to salvage only one hundred before builders moved in and concreted over the site. But I am optimistic about finding another. Thousands await discovery and the best place to begin a search is in a village without a duck pond; it almost certainly had a village pond at some time in its history and there is always a chance that an old resident will have a dim memory of its location. Failing such a site, you should visit every accessible pond in your area. It could well be half full of rare bottles.

Countryside sites

Take an afternoon drive through the rural areas of any county in Britain and you are certain to pass a dozen superb bottle-hunting sites along your route. Country pubs, bridges, fords, old breweries and glassworks can all

23

be found in large numbers in the countryside, and what I have written about libraries, newspapers, rivers, streams, canals and ponds applies as much to the countryside as it does to towns. In your search for old records you will find Rural District Councils as helpful as city dwellers find town halls; and your chats to old people are likely to be even more rewarding. The rustic memory is a long memory and you will soon find a friendly country dweller who can guide you to an excellent old dump. It may be a smaller site than a town dweller might encounter but its bottles will be equally varied and beautiful.

I have found farmers to be particularly helpful in my searches for sites in the country. Many farms have been occupied by the same family for several generations and it is not uncommon to meet a farmer who knows the exact locations of half a dozen dumps on his land and can tell you the periods during which they were used.

Even abandoned farm cottages make fascinating sites for the enthusiastic bottle collector, especially when the site of the cottage's old rubbish dump is unknown and must be located by intelligent detective work. Where would you have dumped the household rubbish if you had lived in

24

the cottage a hundred years ago? Most beginners, especially town dwellers, think of the garden as a likely spot, and it is quite probable that one or two old bottles and jars can be picked up there. But country people were and are generally much tidier in their dumping habits than those who live in towns. Garden dumps are an urban habit acquired by people accustomed to buying their vegetables in shops. The 19th-century farm labourer grew his vegetables in his garden plot and is unlikely to have used this food-producing area for wholesale dumping.

The general practice was to have an empty cart stationed near the kitchen door into which all the household rubbish was thrown. When the cart, which might have been hand or horse-drawn, was full, it was hauled off to the dump for emptying. A group of cottagers might have used one large cart to serve three or four families; but whether for one household or several the practice was generally the same.

Often the route the cart took will be obvious—a narrow track leading from the rear of the buildings to a nearby hollow or chalk pit. If not, the general topography of the area can provide clues to lead you to the dump. It is unlikely that a full cartload of rubbish would be hauled uphill; and a screen of trees or bushes around the site was always desirable. In hilly districts look for the site in hollows not too far from the buildings, and pay particular attention to woods and copses.

Similar abandoned cottages are found in forests, on moorland and in mountainous regions. Sometimes they are farm cottages; sometimes they are associated with long-dead industries such as mining. They are the British equivalents of American ghost towns and always hold rich finds for the bottle enthusiast. In forests, wooden buildings might have rotted away leaving only a rectangular clearing and an overgrown trackway as clues to their former existence. On this type of site look out for nettle patches which often cover old dumps. Nettles love soil which is rich in humus and they grow profusely on top of household rubbish.

On moorland and in mountainous regions, houses were often robbed of their stone-built walls when abandoned and you may come across nothing more than a strip of half wild garden or a row of carefully planted trees to indicate the site of a former house. If the buildings were associated with mining you might find that worked-out mine shafts were used as convenient dumping grounds. Areas beneath cliffs and rocky overhangs are also worth searching.

Ploughed fields can hold many clues and bottles. Hollows which made ploughing difficult were often filled with rubbish and given a covering of two or three feet of soil. Years of ploughing disturb and scatter such dumps across many acres of land, and bottles and jars a hundred or more years old can often be picked up when walking across a newly-ploughed field. The best time to search this type of site is in winter after heavy rain. There will be no crop growth to obscure the surface and rainwater will have washed away soil from surface objects and made them much easier to spot. I know of one man who searched a field which had been used as an old dump and found a superb 17th-century china figure. Unfortunately the head of the ornament was missing, but the man kept it as an interesting find. The following year on the same site he was fortunate enough to find the missing head lying on the surface of the field not far from the spot where he had found the body. He is now the proud owner of a repaired, but valuable, piece of 17th-century china.

Another very profitable method of site-hunting in the countryside is to keep a sharp lookout for trackways, paths and lanes leading from roads. If their entrances are partially overgrown with bushes never pass without checking their routes as they could lead you to a bottle hoard.

Town sites

The best bottle-hunting sites in towns are undoubtedly those uncovered during building and road repair work. However, there are other spots which should be added to your list of possible sites as they can yield good finds.

Your own home might be an excellent place to start a bottle hunt. Town gardens were often used as rubbish dumps in the 19th century and it might be that your front lawn covers a fine collection of Victorian bottles. You will have to dig it up to find the site because bottles do not rise to the surface on lawns as they might on a well cultivated vegetable plot. Occasionally lawns are removed from front gardens and if the house is Victorian or earlier probe rods might reveal bottles two or three feet down.

If you are constantly turning up clay tobacco pipe fragments and pieces of broken glass or pottery in your back garden, a bottle dig could pay dividends. You could be digging up rubbish thrown there by former occupants; or you may have disturbed part of a dump which covered the site long before the house was built. If your house is relatively modern you should research the history of the site on which it was built at your local library or town hall.

Old houses with cellars have provided many new collectors with their first bottles. If your house has a long disused cellar you should make a thorough search for old bottles which may have been stored there. Attics deserve similar attention. Many old and very valuable fruit-preserving jars dating from early Victorian times are to be found neatly stored in cardboard boxes in attics throughout the country.

Even garages and garden sheds can be worth searching if they have not been given a good clean out for a number of years. I have found very collectable bottles in garden sheds and I recommend them as good sites. It might even pay you to offer to clean out old sheds for relatives and neighbours free of charge if you suspect that they might hold bottles.

A vast amount of demolition work goes on in towns and cities all over Britain and if you can befriend a demolition contractor who specializes in houses, you are certain of a never-ending supply of first-class sites. As well as attics, cellars and outbuildings you will be able to search underneath floorboards in downstairs rooms. Here you are sure to find old bottles which were thrown there by the bricklayers and carpenters who built the house. I have found a fantastic variety under floorboards—beers, wines, lemonades, paste jars and even quack medicine bottles. They are almost always in excellent condition because they rarely broke when thrown on to the soft earth which is found under most old houses, and they are really worth seeking.

One other spot I must mention, and which all town dwellers should visit, is the local allotment site. Many allotments cover old dumps and because they are constantly coming under the spade they constantly produce old bottles. It is not uncommon to find heaps of bottles and jars which have been raked out of the soil and stacked around the perimeters of allotments. They are placed there by allotment gardeners who will usually be delighted if you offer to take them away. This is one of the best 'no-digging' methods of collecting bottles that I know and I can thoroughly recommend it as a way of starting a good collection.

When you know the approximate locations of several old dumps, you can turn your attention to recovering some of the bottles they contain; but do bear in mind that wrong recovery techniques could lead to broken bottles, unnecessary hard work and even failure to make any worthwhile finds. The correct methods of recovery are very easy to learn. It is worth grasping a few basic techniques before you start; that way you will be guaranteed more bottles and more pleasure from your first site and avoid possible disappointment.

Clothing

You will need some old clothing capable of throwing off dirt and able to take hard wear. If it has those two basic qualities it does not much matter what you wear so long as you are comfortable and able to remove an outer jacket as the digging warms up. For footwear I recommend a pair of strong shoes or lightweight boots. There is much broken glass on bottle sites and the soles of your footwear must be tough enough to protect your feet from cuts. On river, canal, stream and pond sites, a pair of waist-length waders are essential; a chest-length pair even better. Buy the best you can afford even if it has to be a good second-hand pair. Poor quality waders will not stand up to a season of bottle hunting.

Gloves are another essential requirement. The industrial type sold at surplus stores are ideal for land sites. They should also be worn over long rubber gloves for underwater work. A third pair of thin woollens worn under your rubbers can be a blessing when working in cold water during winter.

Tools

The basic bottle-hunting tool is the narrow garden fork. You should never go bottle hunting without one. Ladies will find a lightweight model less tiring; and everyone should make sure that the fork which they select is neither too heavy nor too long to handle comfortably.

A folding shovel, also on sale at surplus stores, will prove very useful. Buy one with a combination shovel and pick head. The pick is excellent for tackling any stones and rubble you might encounter; the shovel is used to skim the soil in order to locate bottles you have loosened with your fork. In the absence of a folding shovel a small garden spade is quite effective.

There are two essential items which you can either make yourself or buy from a supplier of bottle-hunting equipment. They are the probe rod and the glass-bottomed bucket. Both must be acquired if you are to become a successful bottle hunter.

The probe rod is used to locate underground bottle sites. To make one you require two pieces of half-inch steel rod, one four feet long, the other twelve inches long. A sharp point is made at one end of the longer piece, and the shorter piece is welded to the other end to form a handle horizontal to the pointed shaft. Two rubber grips are then fitted to the handles to provide a comfortable hold. The length of

Equipment

Fig. 6 Tools and equipment for your dig: glass-bottomed bucket, probe rod, plastic tube, fork and folding shovel

the pointed shaft is not critical but four feet is ideal for the average user. Taller readers may find a shaft length of five feet more comfortable in use.

The bucket is made by cutting a round hole in the bottom of a metal waste-paper bin. Make the hole as large as possible but leave a ledge of metal half an inch in width on which the glass will rest. Measure the diameter of the bottom of the bin and ask your local glass merchant to cut a circle of glass to fit this diameter. Waterproof adhesive is then applied to the inside of the ledge you left when cutting the hole, and the glass is lowered onto it from the top. Press the glass down firmly and hammer half a dozen brass panel pins into the outside of the bucket so that they pierce the metal a fraction of an inch above the glass. Now apply waterproof adhesive to the top of the glass to cover the panel pins.

Allow a full day for the adhesive to dry thoroughly before fitting a carrying strap to the top of the bucket. This is made from a strip of webbing long enough to enable you to carry the bucket strapped around your neck. Cut two slots in the top of the bucket, pass the ends of the webbing through them and sew the joints. You now have a glass-bottomed bucket which you can hang around your neck to leave both hands free when working in water.

The glass-bottomed bucket is ideal for hunting bottles in fairly clear water up to three feet deep. For greater depths or muddier water a glass-bottomed tube is far better. This is made from a length of $4\frac{1}{2}$ inch-diameter p.v.c. soil pipe which can be bought in six foot lengths from any builders' merchant. Cut off a length of tube suitable for the depth of water in which you plan to work and secure a circle of glass at one end as you did when making the bucket. You will not have a ledge on which to rest the glass but this can be overcome by using brass panel pins on both sides of the sheet. In use the tube is pushed down into the water until the bottom of the river or pond is visible through the glass.

Bottles are extremely fragile and it is essential that your equipment includes a means of carrying your finds without risk of damage. I use plastic bags with strong handles, lots of paper and several polystyrene ceiling tiles. Each of my bags holds approximately twenty average size bottles and I always pack them with great care. Four or five bottles, each wrapped in sheets of newspaper, are placed in the bottom of a bag and covered with a sheet of polystyrene which has been cut to fit neatly inside the bag. A second layer of newspaper-wrapped bottles is placed on top and another polystyrene sheet added. I fill each bag in this way and add two or three complete newspapers to form a thick cover. The bags can then be carried long distances over rough country without the slightest damage to their contents. I recommend this method of transport, but if you have other suitable containers use them. Materials to avoid are paper carriers which easily become wet in long grass, and cardboard boxes which have a habit of bursting open under the weight of bottles.

You should not overload yourself when setting out on a bottle hunt. If you are going to a land site you will not require your glass-bottomed bucket. Your aim is to collect a fair number of bottles and the less equipment you carry on the outward journey, the more bottles you will manage on the home run. Nevertheless, you should make room for a flask of tea or coffee and a small first aid kit to cope with emergency cuts and bruises.

Permission for your dig

Before we discuss the various sites you will encounter and the different methods used to find bottles on them, we must consider the question of obtaining permission for your bottle hunt from the landowner whose site you plan to visit. It is a most important question so please read carefully.

All land in Britain is owned by someone. If you enter private property without permission you could be guilty of trespass; if you remove any object without the owner's consent you could be accused of stealing that object.

Having made those two points, let me add that in ten years of bottle digging, amateur treasure hunting and rockhounding I have encountered difficulties only twice. On the first occasion I was hunting a very old bottle dump when I strayed onto Ministry of Defence property and was politely ordered to leave by a somewhat apologetic soldier. The second time I had to leave a site unwillingly I had already obtained permission from the owner to make a search for an object I knew to be buried on his land. We had agreed to share the value of the object equally, but before I could locate it the landowner demanded a larger share. I disagreed, he lost his temper, and I was obliged to leave in a hurry.

My hobbies and my interest in objects buried in the ground have taken me to thousands of sites in every part of Britain and those are the only occasions I can recall when I ran foul of landowners. My golden rule has always been: obtain permission before any digging commences, and it has paid dividends. I have met with one or two refusals, but they are far, far outweighed by the number of sites I have worked on with the full consent and approval of their owners.

The majority of sites your research guides you to will be on farm land, waste industrial land and demolition or building sites. On farms, a direct approach to the farmer is best. Try to call on him when he is not too busy and explain fully your interest in antique and old bottles. Tell him you suspect the existence of an interesting dump on his land and show him exactly where it is. If necessary you should seek permission to check the site with a probe rod before you start digging. (See p. 38 for instructions on how to use a probe rod.) So long as the piece of land in question is not under cultivation, and your approach to the farmer is polite, you are almost certain of his approval. Occasionally he will ask you to return later in the year when nearby crops have been harvested; and very occasionally he will refuse to give permission for a dig. Whatever his decision you must abide by it.

On industrial sites, your initial approach should be made in writing to the secretary of the company occupying the land. Points to stress in your letter are that you will not litter the site with rubbish or interfere with industrial equipment. A courteous letter usually meets with approval.

On building and demolition sites where bottles are in

danger of reburial, an approach to the site manager will often result in a quick decision in your favour. Do not get in the way of workmen; do not interfere with surveyors' pegs or machinery; and nobody will object if you remove all the bottles you can carry.

Rivers, canals, streams and ponds are sites on which you also require permission to remove objects. In practice you will find that there is no objection to the removal of old bottles from the water's edge; but on fishing stretches it is essential that you obtain permission before entering the water. You must never trespass on spawning grounds, nor prevent other people from enjoying their hobbies. Approach fishing club secretaries or local river authorities if in doubt. You may find that an offer by you to clean out a stretch of fishing water will be gratefully accepted by a club; in which case you must also be prepared to remove rusty bicycles, tin cans and other objects which might entangle fishing lines.

I have approached a number of river boards and port authorities for permission to search river beds and harbours and I have not had a single refusal. A glance at the letters I received in reply to my requests shows that such bodies invariably stress that interference with navigation, wholesale disturbance of the river bed and trespass on private property adjacent to the river will not be tolerated. If you point out when writing to them initially that you will not commit any of these misdemeanours, permission for your search is almost guaranteed.

I cannot place too much emphasis on the need to leave every site you visit neat and tidy after your bottle hunt. You may wish to contact the same landowner at some future date. If he remembers you as someone who did not leave a mess you will be more than half way to obtaining permission for your next dig. Remember you are an ambassador for all bottle collectors when on a hunt. Act responsibly and we will keep our good name.

One of the first problems you will face as a beginner is that of deciding whether a dump you have located is old

Dating dumps

enough to contain collectable bottles. Modern dumps will be obvious because they contain large amounts of plastic material—detergent bottles, food containers, wrappers—which do not decay. They are not collecting sites and you should not waste your time digging one.

Tin cans are not a certain indication that a dump is modern; though labels which you recognize as modern are reliable clues. The earliest tin cans, which appeared in the 1820s, were hand made. They had a wide-soldered seam down one side and around both ends of the can, and they always carried a large blob of solder in the centre of the lid. This was used to cover the hole made when air was drawn out of the can to create a vacuum inside. Modern cans, which are made by machines, have crimped, solderless joints and no vacuum hole. On many dumps metal objects corrode very quickly and you will be fortunate to find a good example of an early can.

The safest evidence on which to date a dump is the broken glass which is found in abundance on all sites. Nineteenth-century bottle glass contains air bubbles and is almost always coloured—blue, brown, red, amber, white or more commonly a shade of green. Large quantities of colourless glass suggest a modern site.

If you see broken pieces of stone bottles or glass marble mineral waters, the site is obviously worth digging; but not all old dumps contain these highly-prized specimens. Examine any broken bottle tops you see lying around the site. If the majority have an outside thread to take a metal cap, the dump could be modern. Most old bottles were made to take corks and do not usually have threads in their necks. The exceptions are bottles which took a stone cork; but such bottles will have internal, not external, threads.

Beware fly-tipping. This is the practice of dumping modern rubbish on old sites. It happens most often on large sites, but fortunately it is very obvious. Look for unusual mounds on top of the dump. They will either contain building rubble or modern junk, and are a certain indication that fly-tippers have been at work.

Exposed sites were formed by tipping into ravines, over cliffsides and down steep slopes. They are fairly common in the countryside and in coastal regions where this dumping method usually formed a roughly triangular, wedge-shaped site with the oldest material along its base. Above the site you will almost always find an overgrown approach road or trackway. Check this area first for old bottles which might have fallen from carts hauled to the dump along the track. Where there are exposed rocks or tree roots above the dump you might also find bottles which were trapped here when the rubbish was thrown into the ravine.

Digging exposed sites

If these finds indicate that the dump is worth digging you should make a methodical start at the base. Cut a face approximately one yard long and one foot thick into the edge of the dump and after searching the loosened earth start a spoil heap at least one yard to your rear. Cut a second slice from the dump, keeping the face horizontal and making absolutely sure you cut down to the bottom of the site. If you do not do this during the early stages of your dig the exposed face will rise as you progress and you will miss the oldest bottles which lie at the bottom of the site. You will probably dig two or three feet before you start finding bottles, but you should look our for smaller objects, including clay tobacco pipe bowls and pot lids, at this early stage. They often rolled to the edge of the dump during tipping and are likely to be found sooner than heavier bottles and jars.

When you have progressed one yard into the dump and moved all loose soil to your rear, you can use the backfilling method to search the remainder of the site. Work the area left or right of your excavation and rake the soil towards you to fill the space you have already cut out. This is a far easier digging method than carrying all the spoil to a spot behind you and if you work carefully it can be very successful.

Backfilling

Avoid heavy digging with the fork. You will break fewer bottles if you skim the soil carefully with the edge of your shovel after loosening it with the fork. Keep your gloves on and the moment you touch glass stop digging and extract the find by hand. When a dump has been dug by this backfilling method, it is only necessary to replace the first yard or so of soil which you removed when you started the dig to leave a tidy site behind you.

There is a second type of exposed dump which is found along riversides and on building sites. This is the covered dump partially revealed by erosion or trenching operations. It is generally seen as a vertical wall of clay or soil with a layer of dump material as a seam. The seam is darker than the surrounding material with broken glass and pottery fragments along its entire length. Extracting bottles is a simple job. Start at one end of the seam and pull out any unbroken bottles or other finds. The seam will be composed of very loose material and you will have no difficulty in raking out objects to a depth of twelve inches using your pick or the edge of a shovel. Move along the site methodically and resist the temptation to skip unproductive sections because you have spotted a prize find a few yards along the face. The section you miss could hold even rarer hidden bottles. Do not neglect the spoil heap always found near trenches. It may contain many bottles. On riversides where erosion has exposed the seam, the area of bank below the site will probably hold many good finds.

Digging hidden dumps

Pit dumps, depression dumps and others which were covered with a layer of earth when completed, are more difficult to find than exposed sites, but they will contain only collectable bottles because nothing has been added to them since they were covered. They are therefore well worth finding.

A probe rod is used to locate hidden dumps and to define their perimeters. The pointed shaft of the rod is pushed vertically into the ground to indicate the presence of glass below the surface. When the steel rod strikes glass the result is an unmistakable hollow note. Experienced collectors refer to this note as the 'skritch' of steel on glass. If you wish to accustom your ear to the note before setting out on a hunt, bury half a dozen bottles two feet down in the soft earth of

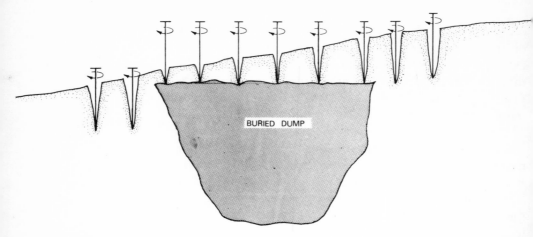

your garden. Tread down the soil until it is well compacted and then push your rod into the ground. As it strikes the bottles you will hear the unmistakable 'skritch' of steel on glass.

Rarely will your research pin-point the exact location of a hidden dump. At best you can hope for one or two clues which will guide you to the general area of the site. From that point you must rely on your own observations and your probe rod. Old pits and quarries which were refilled with rubbish are often revealed by slight depressions which result from the sinking of replaced material and the pressing out of air pockets in the dump. Such depressions remain visible for many years unless the land is heavily ploughed or the topsoil removed by erosion. If such a depression is covered with nettles which thrive on humus-rich soil the site should be probed for buried glass.

Make a start in the centre of the site and push your probe rod vertically downwards. If you strike glass or some other obstruction rotate the shaft of the rod to open up or ream the hole. In this way it is possible to see two or three feet beneath the surface of the site without digging. You should never start a dig on the evidence of a single probe which reveals a buried bottle. The correct procedure is to move one yard left or right of your first hole and push the probe into the ground once more. If this produces the 'skritch' of steel on glass continue to probe at one yard intervals until you find the edge of the site. This will be indicated by the

Fig. 7 Using the probe rod to locate a hidden dump and to define its perimeter. Rotate the rod in the direction of the arrows to ream the hole

absence of glass underground, and I cannot stress too strongly the importance of defining the perimeter. If you start digging without knowing the full extent and area of the site you will bury parts of the dump even deeper by throwing disturbed soil in the wrong places. Continue probing until you have located all sides of the dump with your rod.

A sketch plan of the site will prove useful. Mark the line of your probes on it and also indicate the depths at which you strike glass. Reference to the completed plan will then indicate the area of the dump which has the shallowest covering of topsoil. Start your dig at the perimeter of the site nearest to this area of shallow soil. Throw the soil outside the perimeter line and you will not bury another part of the dump even deeper.

I have found that the best method of digging pit dumps is to remove three or four square yards of topsoil before extracting any bottles. The average depth of topsoil is two feet, and if four square yards are removed you will have space in which to work. If you attempt to remove bottles from a hole only one yard square you will find it difficult to bend and dig in this small space. When you have removed all the bottles you can comfortably reach in the exposed area the backfilling method described earlier should be used to uncover the adjacent part of the dump.

Underwater sites

Hunting bottles in rivers, canals, streams and ponds is an exciting way of building up a fine collection and one which calls for some knowledge of how bottles in water are moved by currents. When you have located a likely hunting ground below an old bridge, near a waterside pub or adjacent to a riverbank dump, you should visit the site with your waders, glass-bottomed bucket and digging fork. Try to get a view of the river from a high vantage point—a bridge or a steep hill are ideal spots—and spend a few minutes looking at the water before you start your bottle hunt.

Any object thrown from a bridge or boat or the water's edge into the middle of a river will travel downstream on a diagonal path which will carry it towards one of the

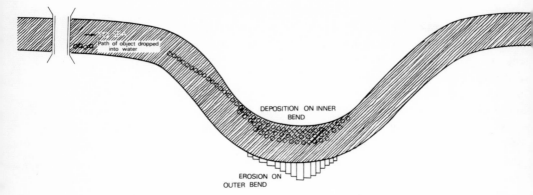

Path of object dropped into water

DEPOSITION ON INNER
BEND

EROSION ON
OUTER BEND

Fig. 8 A river meander
to show how bottles and
other objects will collect
on the inner bend

riverbanks. How far downstream the object will travel, and which bank it will move towards, are determined by the speed of the current and the bends in the river. If, from your vantage point above the site, you can see a bend in the river, make that the starting point for your search. Choose the right bank if the river bends to the right; the left bank if the river swings in that direction, and make your way to the inside of the bend before you enter the water.

When you reach the site you will be on the inside of a river meander. Here, on every river, the current slackens and loses speed. This is because its force is spent eroding the outer edge of the bend, and you will probably be able to see the great swirl of water, or eddy current, which always occurs on river meanders. The current swings around at this point and all movable objects carried by the force of the water are dropped where the power of the flow becomes too weak to transport them further. It is on the inside bend that this occurs.

When you have pulled on your waders and hung the glass-bottomed bucket around your neck, enter the water at a right angle to the bank. Move slowly and carefully; use your fork to feel the bottom. At waist depth, examine the bottom through your bucket. Stand quite still so that your feet do not throw up silt to obscure the view; push the bucket down almost to its lip, and search the area around your feet for bottles. Some will be lying on the surface of the bed, others will be partly buried in mud or

40

gravel and you will have to dig them out with your fork. You will soon get to know the feel of bottles beneath your feet, and this is an excellent way of finding those which are completely buried by mud. Unbroken specimens will roll easily under your sole.

There is a knack in pulling the bottles out of the water without getting your sleeve too wet which can only be learned by trial and error. Move each bottle towards your feet with the fork and trap it between the prongs of your fork and one of your waders. Slowly raise your foot towards the surface keeping the bottle pressed against it with the fork. Grasp it with your hand as soon as you can reach it and place it in your bucket for safety. When you have collected two or three bottles or cleared the area of finds you should leave the water along the same route by which you entered. If you get into the habit of entering and leaving

Fig. 9 The author at work with a glass-bottomed bucket

the water in this way, you will not find yourself stepping unexpectedly into deep holes or tripping over unseen stones.

When you have cleared an area of finds, move upstream a few yards. Mud and silt which you have stirred up by walking in the water will not obscure your vision if you move against the current in this way. In the water you should keep a look out for crevices and holes in the riverbed where bottles are often trapped. It will not be long before your eyes become accustomed to the different world you see through your glass-bottomed bucket, and you will soon become expert at picking out bottle shapes in the mud and shingle.

On tidal rivers you will find many bottles in the stretch of foreshore which is exposed between high and low water. Digging this area can produce many hidden specimens, the glass of which has often become heavily opalized by the mineral content of the mud. This imparts a whitish iridescence to the surface of the bottle which is highly prized by many collectors. Profitable searches can also be made along non-tidal riversides after heavy floods when bottles from deep water will be found on the banks.

Similar search techniques are used on canals and streams. In ponds, where there is no current to carry away silt stirred up by waders, a slightly different method using a glass-bottomed tube should be employed. Start your search by entering the water at one side of the pond. Tread very carefully and disturb the bottom as little as possible. When visibility through the tube becomes so poor that you cannot see the bottom clearly, leave the water and move to the opposite side of the pond. Carry out a similar search here and when you can no longer see in the murky water you will be able to return to the other side of the pond where the silt will by this time have settled once again. By using this search method it is possible to work the entire perimeter of the pond in fairly clear water.

The history of glass is at least as old as ancient Egyptian civilization. Five thousand years ago craftsmen on the Nile fashioned beautiful objects in glass to adorn the tombs of their kings. They made glass from sand, soda and lime in the same way as large amounts of glass are made today; and the secrets of adding beautiful colours to glass were known to them. Three thousand years later the Romans brought glass to Britain, importing large quantities of glassware for decorative and household use. Yet relatively little glass-making was carried on in Britain by the Romans; it was not until the 16th century, more than a thousand years after the departure of the Roman legions, that the manufacture of glass became an important industry.

In the mid-1500s immigrants from Europe, skilled in the manufacture of glass, settled in the south of England. They made window glass and tablewares of all descriptions and they also produced some of the first commercial bottles. These were tiny, narrow-necked vials with tapering sides used by alchemists and apothecaries for their elixirs and medicines. They were usually free-blown and green or aqua in colour.

The usual method of making the glass and producing the bottle was as follows. Sand, potash and lime were mixed together in a crucible of clay and fired in a small rectangular furnace. The potash was obtained by burning wood or bracken; and the wood-fired furnaces were built on steep, sloping ground to catch as much draught as possible. Broken pieces of glass, known as cullet, were also added to the crucible in order to speed the melting process.

When the materials in the crucible had combined chemically to form glass, the molten liquid was cooled slightly until it possessed the consistency of treacle. At this point the glassblower would dip his iron blowpipe into the crucible and take up a small quantity of glass. By blowing down the pipe he would produce a sphere of glass which he then shaped by rolling it on a flat stone or by spinning the rod between his fingers. When he had produced the required shape, the bottle was allowed to cool slightly until it was sufficiently hard to crack or shear from the end of the

3 Dating and identifying your finds

blowpipe. The completed bottle was then placed on a shelf in the flue of the furnace and allowed to cool slowly so that the glass annealed and was thus toughened.

These 16th-century glass furnaces required vast quantities of timber, both as fuel and for the production of potash. On the south coast of England, glassmakers found themselves in competition with other industries, including shipbuilding, which also depended on available supplies of wood, and it was not long before the glass manufacturers moved to other parts of the country. Early in the 17th century, coal-fired furnaces were invented and the glass makers, freed from the need to have vast forests close at hand, concentrated their glassworks in a few large centres, notably London, Newcastle-upon-Tyne, Bristol and Stourbridge. By 1696 there were approximately 40 glassworks with a total annual production of 3,000,000 bottles. Their products were transported to other parts of the country by road, sea and canal, and many bottles were exported. The Bristol glassworks, for example, supplied bottles for mineral waters, beer and cider to the whole of the West Country, and also shipped bottles to Ireland, the West Indies and the American Colonies. English-made bottles have actually turned up in Indian graves in a number of American states. It was not until 1739 that the first important bottle factory was established in America near Salem, New Jersey.

Fig. 10   A Bellarmine jug

Until the 17th century, wines and beers were either drawn from barrels or carried in bottles of stoneware or leather. Much of the stoneware was imported from Europe and many of these salt-glazed bottles made in Holland had a mask or face representing Cardinal Bellarmine, a controversial Italian clergyman who bitterly opposed the Dutch Reformed Church, incised or pressed into their necks. It was a common practice to insult the Cardinal by smashing the bottle bearing his effigy after the wine or beer had been consumed, and fragments of these 16th- and 17th-century bottles are often found on riversides today.

Wine was the first important beverage to be sold in glass bottles. The earliest wine bottles, which appeared in the 1650s, were free-blown and light green in colour. They were much larger than the earlier medicines and their necks and lips were finished in a more professional manner. When the glassblower had produced the sphere of glass on the end of his blowpipe, an apprentice would take a solid iron rod, known as a pontil rod, dip it into the molten glass in the crucible and attach it to the bottom of the sphere. The glassblower then broke off his blowpipe and held the partly-made bottle on the pontil rod. The sheared neck was thrust into the furnace once again and softened. The glassblower then rolled it against a stone or flat piece of iron and flattened the edges of the neck. This produced a much neater lip.

These rolled-lip wine bottles were an improvement on earlier sheared-lip medicines but it was difficult to place them squarely on a table top or shelf because of the jagged scar left when the pontil rod was broken off. They were therefore wrapped in willow basketwork or placed on metal rings which lifted the pontil scar clear of the surface when they stood on a shelf or table, and also provided added protection for the thin glass. Later, when thicker glass came into use, the 'kick-up' was evolved. This was produced by the apprentice who would apply pressure to the pontil rod when he attached it to the bottom of the sphere. This produced an indentation, or 'kick-up', still

Wine bottles

45

found on many modern wine bottles.

Corks in the 17th century were not the air-tight wine bottle corks we use today. The first closures were oiled hemp, but these were soon replaced by wedge-shaped corks. They were quite loose-fitting and many were richly ornamented with silver. To prevent loss they were tied to the neck of the bottle; at first by string, later by brass and copper wire. This was tied around the neck beneath the string ring, a narrow collar of glass added below the lip after the bottle had been made. When flush and tight-fitting corks came into use, following the invention of the corkscrew, the string ring was incorporated into the lip of the bottle both to strengthen the neck and to provide a means of securing the wires which held the cork.

It must be made clear that 17th-century wine merchants did not sell their wines in glass bottles. Their clients, mainly nobility and landed gentry, sent their own bottles to the merchant who filled them with wines from his casks. Glass bottles were status symbols made to individual client's orders at the glassworks. To identify his bottles each owner would have them marked or sealed. This was done by placing a molten blob of glass on the side of the bottle and pressing a metal seal into it before it hardened. The earliest seals were coats-of-arms and other heraldic devices. Later, as glass bottles became more popular, initials, sur-names and even complete sentences were impressed on the seals. By the middle of the 18th century, sales of bottled wines had greatly increased and wine merchants and tavern keepers adopted the idea of putting their own seal on the bottles they sold. The practice died out in the early 1900s when embossing became popular.

The first wine bottles were long-necked with spherical bodies and the only noticeable change in their shape be-tween 1650 and 1700 was a shortening of the neck and a slight flattening of the body to an 'onion' shape. A few had handles, and there were other regional variations. Then, in 1703, a trade agreement which was to change the drinking habits of the upper classes was signed with Portugal. Under this treaty Portuguese wines were imported into England at

1	2	3	4	5

Fig. 11   Evolution of wine bottles. 1—1650; 2—1700; 3—1750; 4—1800; 5—1850

one-third less duty than the wines of other countries; while the duty on English woollen and cotton goods entering Portugal was also cut dramatically. Prior to the signing of this treaty most of the wines consumed in England came from France; but after 1703 more than two-thirds of our wines came from Portugal.

This led to a great change in the shape of bottles. Port is matured in the bottle and to ensure that the bottle remains airtight during the maturing period the cork must remain moist and swollen. To achieve this the bottle is laid on its side, and spherical bottles are quite unsuitable for this purpose. Wine merchants of the period complained that they took up far too much room on shelves and were forever rolling off and breaking. What was needed was a bottle which could be laid on its side safely and which took up as little room as possible. The new bottle which the glass makers designed for this purpose was straight-sided and cylindrical. Those produced between 1710 and 1790 have necks as long as their bodies and they are quite wide at the base with slightly tapering sides. By 1800 necks had shortened and the bottles were much narrower, not unlike the wine bottles of today. (See Fig. 11.)

Case bottles

The favourite drink of the working classes in the 1700s was gin. Vast quantities were imported from Holland and much inferior, home-produced spirit was also sold. It was shipped in wooden cases holding twelve bottles each and a special type of square bottle, known as the case bottle, was produced for this purpose. Unlike the free-blown wines, case bottles were blown in wooden moulds. The moulds were of box-section and had slightly tapering sides to make it easier to remove the blown bottle. The glassblower placed his blowpipe loaded with glass melt into the open-ended box and was thus able to blow a square bottle. Most of the early examples of case bottles to survive have sides which sagged badly after removal from the mould; but the techniques of mould-blowing were soon to improve.

An interesting method of strengthening the necks of bottles was also developed when the early case bottles were made. Before removing his blowpipe from the body, the glassblower would push it inwards in the same way as the apprentice pushed in the 'kick-up'. This produced a double thickness of glass in the neck which was made as short as possible for added strength. It is interesting to note that even today square-shaped bottles are still favoured by a number of gin distillers.

Glass beer bottles did not appear until at least one hundred years after wines, although the discovery that beer could be preserved for long periods in bottles was made before the 17th century. Heavy taxation, both on glass and on beer, coupled with the problems of satisfactory closures for beer bottles, discouraged widespread bottled beer sales until the 19th century.

Beer bottles

Like early wine bottles, the first glass beers were spherical and had long necks which were sealed with tied corks. This shape remained popular throughout the 18th century, but in the 19th century the straight-sided, cylindrical type appeared. Wired-on corks were still used and there were many attempts to devise more satisfactory closures. Various metal clamps which held both cork and stone stoppers had limited periods of popularity. Then, in 1872, the internal screw stopper was invented by an Englishman named Henry Barrett. This became the most popular method of stoppering beer bottles and is still widely used today.

Another very popular closure was the swing stopper

Plate 1 Examples of green, blue, brown and amber glass used for 19th-century bottles. *Left to right:* 1 late-Victorian beer, used mainly for stouts and porters, with an advanced type of applied lip; 2 long-necked cobalt blue caster oil, also used for olive oil and hair restorer; 3 another beer, c. 1890. Brown glass was used mainly for ale; 4 amber beer with crown cork. The first of these bottles were machine-made in 1910, but the unusual embossing on many make them well worth collecting

Plate 2 Colour shades on stoneware. *Left to right:* 1 ginger beer c. 1850 with hand-applied glaze; 2 a late example of glazed stoneware, used until about 1920; 3 bulk ink bottle, common until the intro-duction of fountain pens; 4 white-glazed stoneware was popular throughout Victoria's reign for fish paste jars, salad creams and other household com-modities; 5 this hand-glazed preserves jar was dug from the cellars of a Victorian jam factory in Stratford, London

Plate 3 Mineral water bottles. *Left to right:* 1 flat-bottomed Hamilton; 2 typical internal-screw bottle with stone stopper which superseded Codd's marble-stoppered bottle; 3 half-pint Codd bottle (*see* Plate 4); 4 machine-made crown cork of the early 20th century. Many companies who made these first mass-produced bottles are still in existence

Plate 4 Codd's bottles. There were several hundred 'improvements' to the basic design of Hiram Codd's bottle during its reign of popularity from 1875 to 1920. The Codd family patented 50 modifications. Extremely rare examples have oval marbles

invented in 1875. This enabled the cork to be removed by pressing two wire bales which passed through the cork and locked against the neck of the bottle. The cork could be securely replaced again if necessary when part of the bottle's contents had been consumed. The crown cap, the main rival of the internal screw stopper, was invented by an American named William Painter in 1892.

Mineral water bottles

Artificial mineral waters were first made by an Englishman named Joseph Priestley in 1772 and soon became popular drinks. The earliest beverages were bottled in earthenware, but these were soon replaced by glass bottles for still drinks. The gas pressure inside carbonated drinks bottles tended to loosen corks if they dried out. To overcome this, a round-bottomed bottle, which had to be stored on its side and thus kept the cork moist, was introduced. The earliest was patented by an Englishman named William Hamilton in 1814. This remained popular, particularly for soda waters, until at least 1916. However, it was not until 1872, when the internal screw stopper was invented, that carbonated soft drinks were sold in straight-sided, cylindrical glass bottles.

In 1870, a flat-bottomed version of the Hamilton bottle was introduced. This was also stored on its side, but being flat-bottomed was much easier to fill. Like the Hamilton bottle it had a cork stopper, and it was not until 1903 that it was adapted to take a crown cap. It remained popular until about 1920.

Perhaps the most famous of all unusually stoppered bottles was the glass marble type. It was patented by Hiram Codd,

49

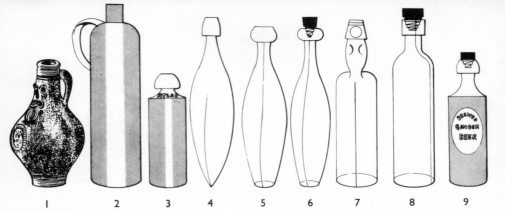

1	2	3	4	5	6	7	8	9

of Camberwell, in 1875. The stopper was an internal glass marble which was forced by the gas pressure inside the bottle against a rubber ring in the neck. To pour out the liquid, the glass marble was pressed down with a wooden cap and plunger supplied with each bottle. The marble was trapped behind two lugs pressed into the neck, thus enabling the bottle to be emptied. There are many variations to be found; most of them prompted by a need to develop a stopper which would not be attractive to small boys who constantly smashed the bottles to recover the marble. Mr. Codd's bottles, or variations of them, were in use from 1875 until 1930 in Britain, and they are still made in other parts of the world today, particularly in those countries which were once part of the British Empire.

The soda water syphon was invented in 1813 by Charles Plinth. Earliest varities had a simple stopcock at the end of a glass tube which passed through the neck of the bottle. Modern types operate on much the same principle but have a spring-operated valve opened and closed by a lever arm. Mineral water bottles are also illustrated in Plates 3 and 4.

Fig. 13 Evolution of mineral water bottles. 1—17th-century Bellarmine Flemish ware jug; 2—18th-century English stoneware; 3—19th-century stone ginger beer; 4—the Hamilton bottle of 1814; 5—flat-bottomed Hamilton of the 1870s; 6 — flat-bottomed Hamilton with internal screw stopper made after 1872; 7—Hiram Codd's glass marble bottle of 1875; 8—1890s internal screw bottle with vertical sides; 9—early 20th-century stone ginger beer

Food bottles and jars

In the latter half of the 17th century the preservation of perishable foods in glass jars began to grow in popularity. The earliest jars were wide-mouthed with flat glass lids which were glued onto the jar after the contents had been boiled. They were used mainly for pickles and sauces which did not require a fully airtight seal. In the early 1800s a Frenchman, Nicholas Appert, developed a glass preserving jar which had a long cork hammered into its neck after the jar had been filled and boiled. This was used by the French navy for some years with great success. Many other closures for preserving jars were tried with varying degrees of success in both the U.S.A. and Britain. Then, in 1858, an American, John Landis Mason, invented the screw-topped jar which popularized home fruit and vegetable preserving in the United States. It was not until the beginning of the 20th century that the practice became popular in Britain with the introduction of Kilner and similar jars.

Milk was first sold in glass bottles in 1884. Goats' milk was the first to be offered to the public in these newfangled containers, which had wired-on stoppers, but they were never popular. In 1894, swing-stoppered bottles were introduced for sterilized milk but they did not achieve wide popularity either; the public still preferred to buy milk from the milkman's churn. It was not until after 1918 that bottled milk became widely used.

Medicines, as already mentioned, were the first products to be sold in commercial containers. Earthenware vases were popular for solid drugs in medieval times, and narrow-necked vials were used for liquids. Case bottles, similar to the early gin bottles, were also used by apothecaries. The early 19th century was a period of massive growth in sales of quack medicines, spa waters, patent hair tonics and other preparations, all of which were sold in glass bottles. Cylindrical, oval, flat and panel shapes were all popular. Cylindricals with ground glass stoppers are still found in chemist's shops today. They were often acid-etched with the name of the contents on the side of the bottle.

Medicine and perfume bottles

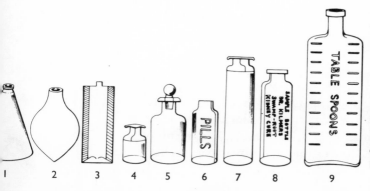

Fig. 14 Medicine bottles. 1—16th-century earthenware; 2—early free-blown flask; 3—case bottle of the 18th century; 4—flared lip; 5—ground glass stopper; 6—early 19th-century sheared lip; 7—3-piece mould cylindrical made after 1820; 8—example of early 19th-century embossed medicine bottle; 9—20th-century medicine bottle

Perfume bottles have a long history, which continues to provide fascinating bottles even today. Since the 18th century a wide range of colours and shapes have been produced. In the late 19th century bottles in the shapes of animals and birds were introduced on a wide scale and today many cosmetics manufacturers have revived the tradition.

Throughout these two or three hundred years of progress in glass bottle manufacture the makers of earthenware containers fought long and hard for their share of the market. Between 1650 and 1850 most wines, spirits and beers made the transition from stoneware to glass containers, though some gins were, and still are, bottled in earthenware flasks. Many ciders and vinegars were sold in stone bottles until well into the 20th century; and stone ginger beers remained great favourites until as late as 1930. When the internal screw thread came into use on glass mineral water bottles in 1872, the stone bottle makers adapted the technique for their bottles and used stone rather than cork stoppers. In Victorian Britain a revolution in the marketing of foods and household products occurred with the growth of large cities and towns. This provided a vast market for earthenware bottles, jars and pots of all descriptions, shapes, sizes and colours.

Bottle manufacturing techniques

Free Blown. As already mentioned, the earliest commercial bottles were free blown on the end of a blowpipe. The craftsman shaped the bottle by rolling the semi-molten glass against a stone or flat piece of iron, and by spinning the rod between his fingers. It was a slow method of making bottles and it was also difficult to make bottles to precise measurements.

Wooden moulds. As demand for bottles grew, a quicker method of producing them had to be found, and moulds were the first step towards mass production. Wooden moulds were not unknown before the development of commercial bottles. Roman mould-blown bottles have

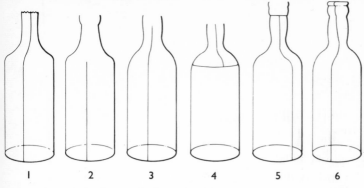

been found; and even before the blowpipe was invented the Egyptians used a cone-shaped mould of clay which was dipped repeatedly into molten glass until a vessel of sufficient thickness was formed around it. The clay was then scraped away to leave a cup-shaped glass vessel.

The wooden moulds of the 18th century were hollowed out of solid timber and were used to form the bodies of the previously mentioned case bottles. The sides of the mould tapered slightly so that the blown glass body could be withdrawn easily when cooled. Shoulders, necks and lips of the early moulded bottles were always hand-formed. With the rise in demand for cylindrical bottles, a hinged, two-piece mould was developed. This enabled the rounded shoulders of the bottle to be formed inside the mould which could be opened to extract the partly-formed bottle. Necks and lips were, however, still hand-made after removal from the mould.

By the beginning of the 19th century most bottles were formed in two-piece wooden moulds; and throughout the early part of this century moulding techniques improved to include bodies of various shapes. Necks and lips were, however, still hand-applied.

Metal moulds. It was around the middle of the 19th century that metal moulds were introduced. They brought much greater flexibility to moulding techniques and enabled shoulders and necks as well as bodies to be formed inside the mould. Some of the bottles were made in three separately formed parts: a body and two identical shoulder and neck sections. The body of the bottle was blown first in a one-piece metal mould, and the sections which formed the

53

shoulders and neck were added before more molten glass was introduced into the mould. These could then be removed when the glass had hardened and an entire bottle, minus only its lip, could thus be completely mould blown.

Strap moulds were often used for whisky flasks and other flat bottles. They produced mould seams only along the edges of the bottle and left front and back faces free of joints which would have made embossing difficult.

The pontil rod and the jagged scar it left on the bottom of the bottle also began to disappear around 1850. On some bottles made without a 'kick-up', the pontil had earlier been ground flat; but now a snap clamp which held the sides of the hot bottle while the lip was being applied was introduced and the pontil rod became obsolete. There were other mould variations. Four-piece moulds were not unknown, and rarer multiple-mould bottles have been found. Another technique, known as turn moulding was employed to eliminate mould seams by coating the inside of the mould with soap, beeswax and sawdust. Bottles made by this method were rotated, or turned, inside the mould while the glass was still in a molten state. The heat reduced the added materials to a smooth carbon lining on the inside of the mould. Although these bottles display no mould seams they are easily distinguishable from much earlier free-blown bottles by their uniformity of shape. Free-blowns are always irregular in body shape, neck angle and 'kick-up'.

Lips

Sheared lips were the earliest and simplest type. They were made when the blowpipe was cut or sheared from the blown bottle and they remained in use for certain bottled products until the early years of the 20th century when bottles were all mould- or machine-made. It was found that non-fermenting liquids such as inks and syrups which could be stoppered with a loose-fitting cork were ideal for bottling in these easily and inexpensively mass-produced sheared-lip bottles. The jagged edges of the neck left when the blowpipe was snapped off bit into the cork to provide a perfectly secure seal.

Rolled lips were formed by pressing the re-heated neck of the bottle against a flat surface to remove the jagged sheared lip. This type of lip was well suited to bottles which might be used as drinking vessels, such as wines and beers.

Flared lips were used on the earlier medicine bottles. They were also formed by pressing the re-heated neck against a flat surface until it flared outwards. Later a pouring lip was added to facilitate the measuring of medicines one drop at a time.

The *laid-on-ring* was another method of producing a speedy and neat finish to the lip of a newly blown bottle. A ring of molten glass was laid around the sheared lip. This provided a flat ledge for replaceable corks of the type which did not require a corkscrew for their removal. It was popular for medicines and glass-stoppered sauce bottles.

Applied lips with internal screw threads came into use on beer bottles in 1872. They were moulded onto the bottle after the neck and body had been formed and are easily distinguished from later, integrally moulded types by examining the bottom of the lip. On applied lip bottles the molten glass of the lip has a crude, irregular finish and has often run down the neck like melted candle wax.

Applied lips for corked mineral water bottles are known to bottle collectors as 'blob tops'. This accurately describes their appearance. They are thick, bulbous blobs of glass

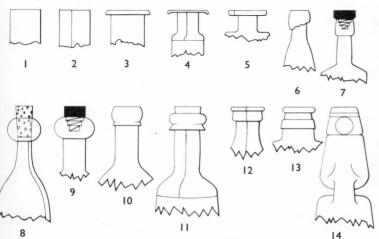

Fig. 16 Lips. 1 — free-blown; 2—sheared; 3—rolled; 4—flared; 5—laid-on ring; 6—applied; 7—internal screw; 8—'blob-top' to take cork stopper; 9—'blob-top' to take internal screw stopper; 10—improved applied lip on 2-piece mould bottle; 11—improved applied lip on 3-piece mould bottle; 12—20th-century lip; 13—collar below lip; 14—Codd's bottle

applied to the neck of the bottle to provide the extra strength needed to take the tight-fitting cork. They are best seen on the Hamilton bottles made before 1903. 'Blob tops' with internal screw threads were also produced after 1872.

Crown lips, designed to take the crown caps now found on most beer bottles, will be obvious because of their uniform shape. Crown-capped bottles were among the first to be made completely in automatic bottle-making machines which began to come into use after 1900. Machine-made bottles can be readily distinguished from hand-finished specimens by examining the mould seams. On machine-made bottles the seam extends along the entire length of the bottle from base to lip. Such bottles should not be entirely dismissed by collectors because many are richly embossed, quite rare, and well worth collecting.

Another very important point to bear in mind when dating bottles by mould seams and lips is that the various transitions and improvements did not take place overnight. In many places, outdated production methods were used for years because the costs of new moulds or new machines were prohibitive; and sometimes because the craftsmen themselves preferred the older methods.

Embossing became possible in the 19th century because of **Embossing**
the introduction of hinged moulds. Metal plates with raised letters were placed inside the mould and when the body of the bottle was blown an embossed impression of the words was formed on the glass. Some of the earliest embossed bottles carried only the name of the contents, or the name of the brewer, merchant or chemist who sold the bottle. It was not long, however, before business-minded people realized the advertising potential of embossing. Patent medicine manufacturers were soon placing orders with glassworks for bottles embossed with fantastic claims for their products. Wine merchants, tavern keepers and mineral water manufacturers were not slow to copy the idea, and by the 1890s seventy-five per cent of all bottles were embossed.

Fig. 17 Examples of 19th-century embossing can be clearly seen on a Lipton's tea bottle and a flat-bottomed Hamilton used for mineral water

Even the 16th- and 17th-century sealed wine bottles were copied, though it is easy to distinguish embossed seals from true sealed bottles. The latter were impressed into a blob of molten glass added to the bottle after it was made; whereas moulded seals were an integral part of the blown bottle. When the pontil scar disappeared after the introduction of the snap clamp, the bottoms of bottles were often embossed; mainly by the glassmakers themselves who began to place batch numbers, order numbers or their own names on the bases of the bottles they made.

The manufacturers of earthenware bottles had used incised and impressed marks and decorations on their wares for centuries. In the late 1900s they began to use transfers on ginger beers, pot lids and many other containers in an effort to compete with the printed labels which by that time were slowly replacing embossing on glass containers.

The early bottle makers were not greatly troubled by the fact that their glass was of a poor quality and badly coloured. Impurities in the raw materials they used, particularly the iron oxide present in the sand, produced light green glass which was quite suitable for the wine bottles of the 17th century. Makers of flat window glass required a finished product with as little colour as possible, and they used only the best quality materials and added manganese to the melt to produce colourless glass.

As more and more products were sold in bottles, demand for glass of a deeper green increased because it was found that light action on some products, particularly alcoholic beverages, produced unsightly sediments in the bottles. To overcome this, glass makers added even more iron oxide to the sand and produced dark green glass. Even larger amounts of iron oxide produced brown glass, and brown bottles were used first for poisons and for medicines. Black glass, popular for beers in the 19th century, was also produced by adding iron oxide to the crucible; and sometimes by adding carbon in the form of coal or charcoal.

Blue glass, also often used for poisons, was first produced by adding cobalt to the melt. This produced a rich, deep blue. For a lighter blue, copper oxide was used. In fact, copper oxide was probably the most versatile colouring agent at the disposal of the glassmaker. By varying the amount added to the crucible and by carefully controlling the furnace temperature it produced blue, light red and emerald green glass.

White, or milk, glass was very popular in the 19th century for cosmetics. It was made by adding either tin or zinc oxide to the melt, and it remains a popular colour for face cream jars today. Sulphur, silver and chromium were all used to produce various shades of yellow glass, mainly for perfume bottles.

Ruby red was the rarest, and most expensive, glass. It was made by adding an ounce of gold to sixty pounds of glass melt and was only rarely used for commercial bottles. Ruby red glass made today does not contain gold. It is produced by adding selenium to the melt.

Demand for *clear glass* bottles grew in the 19th century when products such as milk, jam, pickles and other foods were first bottled. Manganese was used to produce the earliest colourless bottles and this was a particularly fortunate choice for today's bottle collectors. When bottles made with manganese are exposed to ultra-violet light they turn a beautiful shade of amethyst. In the sunnier climates of America and Australia it is only necessary to place manganese glass in direct sunlight for a few weeks to produce this purple effect. In Britain far quicker results are achieved by the use of an ultra-violet sunray lamp. Most colourless bottles made before 1920 contain manganese in varying amounts. The greater the amount, the deeper will be the shade of amethyst produced. Colourless bottles made since 1920 do not contain manganese. Selenium is the substance now used to produce these bottles and they will not turn purple no matter how long you expose them to ultra-violet light, although in very hot countries they do occasionally turn a yellowish gold if they contain large amounts of selenium.

Chemistry of coloured glass

Substance added to melt	Colours produced
Iron oxide in sand	Light green, or aqua
Additional iron oxide	Dark green
Even more iron oxide	Brown, black
Carbon, as coal or charcoal	Brown, black
Tin or zinc oxide	White, or milky
Gold	Ruby red
Copper oxide at varying kiln temperatures	Red, emerald green, light blue
Cobalt	Deep blue
Manganese	Clear glass which will turn amethyst if exposed to ultra-violet light
Selenium	Clear glass, red
Sulphur, silver or chromium	Yellow

Stone ginger beers, stone ink bottles, preserves jars and many other earthenware containers found in dumps provide a wide variety of colours. White and brown are common, later ginger beers are often two-tone and multi-coloured pot lids can also be found.

Bubbles, tears and stretch marks   No two 19th-century bottles are exactly alike. They may be the same size, the same colour and have identical embossing; but the air bubbles in the glass make each bottle quite unique. The reason for the bubbles is that the glassblower collected the molten glass on the end of his blowpipe from the top of the crucible. In doing so he also collected tiny pockets of gas which were being driven off from the melt by the intense heat. Later production methods removed most of the impurities and gases from the glass before the bottles were made; and the molten glass was also taken from the centre of the crucible to reduce further the possibility of bubbles in the finished product.

Blowing the bottle often elongated some of the bubbles. These are known as 'tears' to bottle collectors and a bottle with lots of tears is highly prized. The forming of the neck sometimes produced stretch marks in the glass which are seen as elongated striations in the glass. Once again, such bottles are sought after by many collectors.

Glazes applied to early stoneware were also hand-applied and this makes every stone jar or pot unique. On many specimens the fingerprints of the man who applied the glaze can be seen in the finished product.

How you clean your bottles is determined to a large extent by where you find them. Bottles from many dumps require nothing more than a quick rinse in clean water to restore them to perfect condition; others will be thickly encrusted with iron stain and will require careful and diligent attention before they are ready for your display shelves.

Whatever the condition of your newly found prizes there is one basic cleaning rule which you must always observe. Never attempt to clean a bottle immediately after digging it out of the ground or pulling it from the mud of a river. You must allow at least twenty-four hours for glass and stoneware to adjust to above ground temperatures and atmospheric conditions. Necks will almost certainly crack if you do not do this because of the stresses caused by the sudden change of environment. Meanwhile, you can collect the equipment you will need for the various cleaning operations.

Equipment

A bath is the first essential item. The best are those large tin ones popular about fifty years ago, but they are very difficult to come by. I make do with a baby bath which my daughter grew out of a year ago. It holds approximately fifty bottles, is suitable for most of my cleaning jobs and being plastic is lightweight and easy to store. A friend of mine uses a large inflatable dinghy, swearing that he has never once cracked a bottle against its air-filled sides.

Other requirements are several pounds of household soda, two plastic buckets, some soft builder's sand, and a couple of pounds of fine gravel. Equipped with these items and a pair of rubber gloves you will be able to clean most bottles from your digs, but very badly stained specimens should be set aside for the special treatments described later.

Cleaning

Half fill your bath with cold water and add a pound of soda, stirring until it dissolves. Next, take your two plastic buckets and fill one with water. Pour a second pound of soda into the other bucket and top up with water. Now give the first bottle a quick rinse in the bucket of clean water to remove loose dirt, and then place it in the bucket containing the soda solution. Make sure it fills completely

61

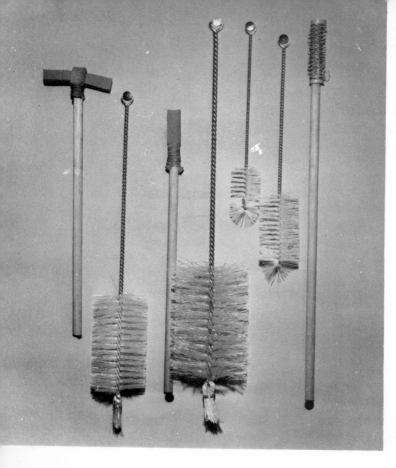

Fig. 18 Cleaning equipment

and place your thumb over the lip before putting the bottle carefully into the bath. By doing this you will ensure that air, which might prevent the soda solution reaching the internal walls of the bottle, is not trapped inside. Continue this procedure, topping up the soda bucket as you go, until the bath is full.

A two-day soak in the bath should be adequate for most bottles. Check by removing one or two after forty-eight hours. Rinse them in clean water and look carefully for stubborn grime. Particularly dirty bottles might require a week in the soda bath to remove all dirt.

It is impossible to remove every stain by this method. Any stains which remain after a full week in the soak must be dealt with by other methods. Remove all the bottles from the bath and set aside those which require further treatment. The soda solution in the bath should be retained. It will clean many more bottles before it becomes too dirty to be of further use. Set aside the stained specimens and rinse your clean ones under running water. Allow them to dry in the open air if possible as this saves the trouble and risk of drying each bottle with a cloth.

If the stubborn stains on the remaining bottles are on the outside of the glass fill one of your buckets with soft sand. Take each bottle by its neck and thrust it into the sand. Rotate it for a few seconds and this should loosen the stain sufficiently for it to be completely removed by washing in clean water.

Internal stains are removed by pouring a handful of gravel into the bottle and adding a small amount of water. Hold your thumb over the lip and shake the bottle vigorously for a few moments. The abrasive action of the gravel

Fig. 19—Cleaning the outside of a bottle in a bucket of sand

Fig. 20 Internal cleaning using fine gravel

will remove most internal staining. Wash the bottle in clean water and it should now be ready to join your other cleaned specimens.

Iron stains To remove internal iron stains first fill the bottle with rust remover and allow it to remain in the bottle for a day or so. If this is followed by the gravel and water treatment the stain will probably disappear. If on the outside of the glass, they can be dealt with by first softening them with a piece of cotton wool soaked in one of the proprietary rust removers sold at most car accessories' shops. Once softened they can usually be completely removed by a further soaking in soda solution. Never use abrasive materials in an attempt to remove stubborn stains. Cleaning bottles with soap-impregnated steel wool pads usually result in badly scratched bottles. The nylon pads which now seem to be replacing steel wool are often useful.

Chemical stains Internal stains on medicine bottles are by far the most difficult to tackle. A long soak in the soda bath will soften and even remove certain chemical stains; but others will resist both soda and rust removers. There is no cleaner which will remove all stains from all medicine bottles without damage to the glass and you must experi-

Plate 5 Makers' marks on stoneware. The earliest examples had incised patterns like that on the second from the left

Plate 6 A bottle display showing the wide colour range and variety of shapes available

Plate 7 A display in a public house. Many publicans are avid bottle collectors; this one specialises in beers

Plate 8 Four unusual inks. *Left to right:* 1 pale cobalt blue sheared lip; 2 'bell' ink; 3 fluted ink. Many examples have ribs on the side which held pen nibs given away free with each bottle; 4 copper-blue ink

ment to find the best cleaner for each stain.

Liquids sold for removing stains from clothing will usually clean tar and resin-based stains from glass, and they are sometimes successful on oil-based stains. Acids are worth trying in extreme cases but they must be handled with great care. It is far better to remove a stubborn stain by a very long soak in a weak acid than it is to try a strong acid in the hope of a quick result. The effect of the strong acid on the glass could spoil it forever. Household bleaches are a safer bet if weak acids fail.

Brushes Nylon brushes used for cleaning babies feeding bottles are excellent for old bottles of a similar shape, but modifications are often necessary. The wire handles on these brushes can easily be extended with dowel rod or additional wire and they can then be used to clean tall bottles. Old tooth brushes can also be pressed into service; some collectors make their own brushes from discarded clothes brushes which they cut up and attach to pieces of wire or wood. Brushes to avoid are those with metal tufts, which scratch glass very easily.

For cleaning glass marble bottles an excellent brush can be made from two or three nylon hair rollers. They should be cut vertically and wrapped and tied around a thin piece of cane. This can then be worked between the narrow shoulders of the bottle and will reach difficult-to-get-at areas very well.

Iridescence This rainbow-like colouring usually found on long-buried aqua glass is not affected by soda solutions, but strong acids should never be used on bottles displaying particularly beautiful iridescence. It is far better to allow small stains to remain rather than risk spoiling a fine specimen by harsh cleaning in an effort to get rid of it.

Opalescence This milky-bluish colouring often found on bottles which have been buried in mud is a scale which can be removed by nylon bristles. In America, collectors prefer not to remove opalescence, whereas most British collectors do so. It is a matter of personal choice.

65

Experimental cleaning methods Cleaning is a controversial subject with all collectors. Everyone has his or her pet theory about the best way to clean this or that bottle. It will not be long before you discover your own particular miracle-worker if you experiment with such things as floor cleaners, biological washing powders, potassium carbonate, burned seaweed and the many other cleaners I have seen used by collectors. The only advice I can offer on experiments is that you should try them first on cracked or duplicate bottles. If you try out your latest miracle-cleaner on a rare find you may regret it.

Stoneware

This can be treated in much the same way as glass, but do take extra care with ginger beer bottles and other items which have transfers and not embossing on their surfaces. If the glaze is in a poor condition, acids can play havoc with the dyes used in the transfers. Luckily a stoneware container need only be thoroughly cleaned on its outside surface. Insides usually need only a wash in warm soapy water.

Final polishing

The appearance of bottles and jars can be greatly improved by a final polish. By far the best substance for imparting that superb polish to your finest specimens is *cerium oxide*. It is a reddish powder which can be bought at lapidary shops and is normally used for polishing semi-precious stones. Bottles should be perfectly clean before you polish them and the best method of applying the polish is on a piece of soft felt. Moisten this with water and sprinkle on a small amount of the powder. Rub it over the surface of the bottle using small circular movements until the entire bottle has been treated. Continue polishing for about ten minutes and keep the pad moist. Then rinse off under running water and you should have a superbly polished bottle worthy of any collector's shelves.

A less expensive method of adding a final polish to newly cleaned bottles is to rub a few drops of light machine oil over the surface of the glass when it is completely dry. This will give the bottle a shine which will last for several weeks; whereas the polish achieved with cerium oxide is permanent.

Once you have visited half a dozen sites and seen for yourself the vast range of bottles there are to collect, you will almost certainly think about specialization. It is something almost every collector does eventually; but I urge you not to make a decision on which particular variety of bottles you will collect too soon after your initial introduction to the hobby. Many newcomers make this error. Knowing little or nothing about the history of bottles, they think only of the popular types such as glass marbles and stone ginger beers which they have seen on sale at antique stalls, and they often miss or neglect far better finds.

I have seen newcomers throw aside rare three-piece mould beers to grab easily recognizable glass marbles; I have watched them reject superbly embossed machine-made bottles because they were under the impression that any bottle with a through-the-lip seam was uncollectable; and I once picked up a fine Bellarmine jug top thrown away on a riverside by someone only interested in stone ginger beers.

Of course, lack of display and storage space inevitably means that you must decide at some time which bottles you are going to take home, clean, polish and add to your collection. Some bottles must always be left behind, but please do not make your decision after two or three digs because you are almost certain to regret it later. Aim at first to find several examples of all types of bottles and jars and if possible put off your decision about specialization for several months. Handle, study, clean and live with as many varieties as possible before you begin to consider which give you the most pleasure.

Until that day I recommend that you visit as many dumps as you can find and extract a few specimens from each. You should always make careful notes on dump locations; and, as your knowledge of bottles increases, you should also carefully record the types and manufacturing dates of bottles found on different sites. This information will prove invaluable in later months when you decide to collect only special bottles. Reference to the notes you have made on

5 Collecting and displaying

Record-keeping

sites visited will provide clues to which of these dumps are most likely to contain the bottles you have become most interested in finding.

Once you do make your decision on which bottles you will collect as a specialist, you should carefully catalogue every variety you find. The British Bottle Collectors' Club, an organization all serious collectors should join, keeps detailed files on bottles found by members all over Britain. The accuracy of these records depends on individual members supplying detailed information about each new variety located, and it is in every member's interests to keep the files up to date. Information required for this central file includes colour, mould marks, embossing, type of lip, a photograph or sketch, where found and any unusual characteristics. As a member you can, of course, use the files for research on the particular branch of the hobby which most interests you.

You may find other collectors living in your area, or you may meet them by becoming a member of The British Bottle Collectors' Club. This will provide you with excellent opportunities to exchange your duplicate bottles and to meet fellow enthusiasts. If you meet another collector who is interested in different types of bottles to those which you have specialized in it is often possible to make a reciprocal arrangement to look out for the other collector's particular requirements. Some collectors also exchange site locations with fellow enthusiasts, each digging an agreed number of bottles from the other's dump. One big advantage of this type of arrangement over exchanges by mail is that it saves heavy postage expenses and reduces breakage risks.

There are bottle collectors' clubs in other countries and exchanges of finds and information go on all the time. Regular shipments of bottles, old newspapers, magazines and letters pass between British and American collectors, and I know of a number of collecting friends who have made similar arrangements with collectors in Australia.

Exchanging bottles

Coloured bottles (see Plate 1) are a popular field for the specialist. Cobalt blues are most sought after, though the

Collecting for colour

lighter, copper blues are also much in demand. Most of the blues were poison bottles and cleaning is often difficult. There is little danger from the toxic liquid the bottle might have held since this will almost certainly have evaporated long ago, but sticky residues often remain inside the bottle. It is probably wise to take a little extra care when cleaning old poison bottles. Always wash your hands thoroughly after a cleaning job which should not, of course, be carried out over the kitchen sink.

Browns, both poisons and beers, provide many shapes, shades and sizes. I have seen one or two brown glass marbles, though they are quite rare and you will have to be patient before you can add one to your collection if brown is your favourite colour. Luckily there are sufficient varieties of brown beers to keep most collectors very busy. Yellows, usually sulphur coloured, are most likely to be perfumes. Selenium, the substance used nowadays to produce colourless glass, can produce sun-yellowed specimens in hot climates, but they are very rare in Britain. Those seen in other collectors' displays have usually come from abroad, the best way of obtaining them.

For collectors who do not own an ultra-violet lamp, swapping with collectors in countries with sunnier climates is an excellent means of obtaining amethyst-coloured glass which is fairly common in those areas. The Americans have lots of amethyst glass but very little in the way of earthenwares, and many Americans will be only too pleased to exchange a sun-coloured glass bottle for a stone ginger beer.

You will have a small collection indeed if you decide to specialize in ruby red bottles. They are extremely rare and worth their weight in the gold they contain. Some of the modern reds coloured with selenium are worth collecting for their variety of shape, but there are few embossed examples. The early light reds produced by the addition of copper oxide to the melt are often embossed and very beautiful.

There are so many shades of green to be found in old bottles that you will have to limit your collecting to a few particular shades if that is your chosen colour. There are some excellent dark green beers, richly embossed and full of bubbles, to be found in many dumps. The emerald greens produced with copper oxide are harder to find.

This is another excellent field for specialization and one which is so vast it must be divided into many sub-groups. Pumpkin seeds are a very popular shape. They are those round, flat, long-necked bottles popular in the 19th century for whisky, syrups, and medicinal preparations. They come in many sizes from miniatures to half gallons, and were in use long before the introduction of automatic bottle-making machines. Early varieties are quite round in body shape; later machine-made types have sloping shoulders. Most are colourless or aqua-green but blues and light browns can be found. Unfortunately there are few embossed types.

Coffin flasks, so named because their body shape is reminiscent of old-fashioned coffins, were often used for whiskey. Many are richly embossed and most of the pre-1900 specimens are strap-sided. Like many colourless pumpkin seeds, clear glass coffin flasks will often turn amethyst under ultra-violet light.

Collecting for shape

Fig. 21 This corner of a collector's display shelves illustrates the wide variety of shapes found in old bottles and jars

Few collectors will turn away from a glass marble mineral water when it turns up on a dig. Even if they do not collect them they know they are certain of a good swap if nothing else. As already mentioned, the glass marble stopper was invented by Hiram Codd in 1875. The well-known phrase, 'Codd's wallop', originates from the contempt strong beer drinkers of the day showed for the mineral waters bottled in Codd's invention. There are some superbly embossed varieties from the early 20th century, all in a very pale green glass. Browns are rare and colourless varieties almost unknown in Britain. Those still made abroad are usually in clear glass, but it is selenium glass and will not purple under the sun's rays. Few of the many variations and improvements made to Codd's original stopper seem to come to light. I have seen many different neck crimpings, but none of the oval and other oddly-shaped marbles which were used in an effort to discourage small boys from breaking the bottles for the coveted glass spheres.

I like sheared-lip bottles very much. They do not seem to attract newcomers to bottle collecting and I feel they deserve much more attention. There is little colour variety but some of the embossing is quite beautiful.

Pickle jars and other wide-mouthed containers are rich in variety of shape. Only poor quality glass was used for these very inexpensive containers and it is usually full of bubbles and tears. One particular type, the cathedral jar, has six sides and is most elegantly shaped. Jam jars are another field where there seems to be little competition yet plenty of variety to be found. Preserves jars, usually complete with ingenious clamps and wire bails, are very popular with American collectors and seem to be catching on in Britain.

There are many other bottles and jars well worth collecting for shape alone—Hamiltons, both round- and flat-bottomed, demijohns, cylindricals—the varieties are endless and I leave the final choice to you.

Collecting for embossing

This is the richest field for all collectors and one which provides some of the most beautiful examples of bottle-making craftsmanship. The earliest embossed bottles carried only makers' names, but soon highly ornate trade marks were added to many wines, beers and mineral waters. Look out for those embossed with such phrases as, 'Half penny deposit charged' or 'This bottle must be returned'. They are much in demand by many collectors.

Quack medicines provide some of the most amusing embossing. 'Glycerine and Cucumber', 'Celery, Beef and Iron', 'Prickly Ash Bitters', 'Swamp Root Kidney Cure' and many more will often turn up in a single dump. Hair preparations were sold in richly-embossed bottles and Victorian charlatans made fortunes from hair balsams, dyes, renewers, invigorators, restorers, nourishers, lotions, washes, preservatives, unguents, growers, oils and pomades. One of the oddest embossed medicines I have seen was a small sheared-lip cylinder. It bore no trade mark or maker's name and was simply embossed, 'For Bad Legs'.

One very specialized field in embossed bottles is those rare bottles with errors in the spelling or lettering. The best example I have seen was a glass-stoppered sauce with the word embossed as 'ƧAUCE'. Others have letters missing from the ends of words because the metal plates were wrongly positioned in the mould when the bottle was blown. There are very few to be found, so do not expect a large collection if you limit yourself to these mistakes in glass.

Collecting special containers

There are many collectors who limit their displays to bottles and jars used for one particular product. Beers are one example. The field is vast and you must expect to travel to many different locations to find bottles from breweries from other areas, although a fairly comprehensive collection can be built up by exchanging with other beer specialists. Not surprisingly, many collectors of old beer bottles are publicans. The bottles make superb bar displays (see Plate 7).

Ink bottles (see Plate 8) are also firm favourites with specialists and many types can be found in every dump. Inks were some of the last bottles to be made with sheared lips and they were always made from poor quality glass

Fig. 22 A Victorian advertisement for 'Mellin' Emulsion', a tonic for 'weakness of all kinds'

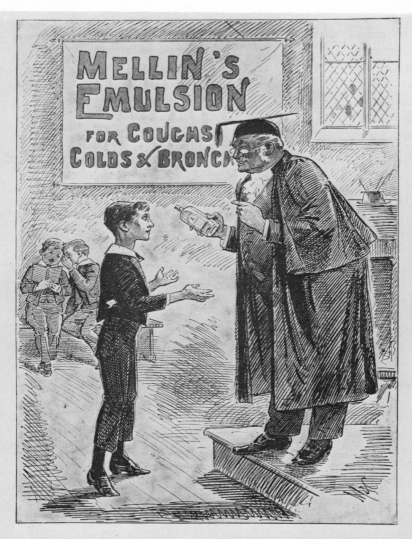

MELLIN'S EMULSION
OF COD LIVER OIL AND HYPOPHOSPHITES.
The Great Strengthener of Chest and Lungs.

VERY PALATABLE AND MOST EASILY DIGESTED.   FOR CHILDREN AND ADULTS.

THE BEST GENERAL TONIC IN WASTING DISEASES, INDIGESTION, AND WEAKNESS OF ALL KINDS.

Price **2/6** and **4/6** per Bottle. Sample Size **1/-** Of all Chemists and Stores, or direct for 5d. extra.

Samples, Pamphlet and Prospectus post free on application to MELLIN'S FOOD WORKS, PECKHAM, LONDON, S.E.

73

with lots of bubbles and tears. Greens and blues are the commonest colours. Shapes include octagonals, triangulars, fluteds, bells, oblongs, squares and one delightful specimen with a slot in the side which held a free nib supplied with every purchase.

Ginger beers are probably the most popular special containers with collectors of stoneware. Those with incised or pressed trade marks and brewers' names are oldest; while the later transfer marked varieties are often dated.

There are many collectors who specialize in different types of moulded bottles. Three and four-piece moulded bottles can be found as beers, medicines and miniature poisons; two-piece moulds were used for every type of bottle; and those rare multiple moulds were usually reserved for perfumes. I have also seen many fine collections of applied lips, 'blob-tops', 'kick-ups' and paste jars.

These few pointers will, I hope, provide you with some ideas on starting your own specialized collection. Do not be influenced too much by my suggestions. Specialized collecting is a very personal matter and your ultimate choice must depend entirely on which bottles or jars give you most pleasure and satisfaction.

Other suggestions

How you display your bottles is equally a matter of personal preference. The few suggestions I would like to make should be used only to stimulate your own creativity. In small rooms bottles look best on a single shelf high up on a wall facing a window. In large rooms they can make beautiful room dividers when set out on one of those instant shelving systems on sale at do-it-yourself stores. I have also seen some excellent outdoor displays with bottles lining garden walls or lawn borders. Stone ginger beers make fine ornaments on sideboards and on small corner shelves; and blue glass always looks its best if light falls on the bottles from behind.

Displaying your bottles

Beautiful vases and unusual ornaments can be made with single bottles. There is a bottle cutter on the market which

Ideas for single bottles

74

Fig. 23 A simple display like this can be most effective

can be used to make drinking glasses, ash trays, table lamps and candlesticks from old bottles.

A ship-in-a-bottle may be beyond the modelling talents of the average collector, but many models-in-bottles are child's play. Select a short-necked, unembossed bottle with fairly clear glass and buy two or three plastic toy soldiers which are fractionally shorter in height than the width of the bottle. Drop the soldiers in boiling water for ten seconds and remove them with tweezers. They will then be soft and pliable and if you work quickly you will be able to squeeze them through the neck of the bottle. Fill the bottle immediately with cold water and the model soldiers will re-harden. Now pour out the water and place the bottle neck downwards in a warm, dry spot for two or three days. When all the water has evaporated off take a piece of wire long enough to reach the bottom of the bottle and you will be able to move the soldiers around inside the bottle and negotiate them into standing positions. A blob of quick-drying glue can then be applied to the base of each soldier in turn. It takes some practice to get all three soldiers correctly positioned but the finished model is worth the effort. As you become more experienced at bottle modelling you might try backgrounds made from paper or strips of balsa wood which can be painted and glued into position.

There are some excellent plastic model kits on the market which can provide material for the enthusiastic modeller. With a few modifications to shape and assembly instructions, most of the miniature sailing ships can be bottled. A Victorian paddle steamer in a Victorian bottle looks perfect. Aircraft can sometimes be fitted into square bottles, but do check the wingspan before you start. Those larger-scale standing figures of kings and queens can be squeezed into tall wines with a fair amount of patience; and half a dozen make a fine 'bottled history' display easily carried from room to room.

Money boxes are also quite easy to make from stoneware bottles with the aid of a silicon carbide wheel and an electric drill. Early attempts should, of course, be made on duplicates or chipped specimens. Simply cut a slot wide enough to take a fifty-penny piece in the shoulders of the jar.

Readers who are interested in lapidary will probably own a tumble-polishing machine. Beautiful imitation gems can be made in a tumbler by using broken pieces of coloured glass instead of pebbles to load the barrel. Grinding times will be approximately half the time it takes to grind quartz. Cabochon rings can also be made from broken pottery fragments picked up on old dumps. Grind them to fit ring bases on your silicon carbide wheel and glue them with 'Araldite'. These small pieces of colourful china and pottery fragments can also be used to make beautiful bracelets and pendants.*

* See *Pebble Polishing* by Edward Fletcher (Blandford Press, 1972).

Many other objects turn up on every bottle dig. On my last site I found a very early electric light bulb with a pontil scar, the arm of a Victorian china doll, several keys, one coin, a dozen glass bottle stoppers, two stone lemonade bottle stoppers, a lead soldier, two very nice toothpaste jar lids, a dozen clay tobacco pipe bowls as well as plenty of bottles and jars. All glass, earthenware, pottery and china survives almost indefinitely in rubbish dumps; whereas metal objects corrode within relatively short times. Iron objects have by far the shortest dump life, closely followed by lead and pewter. Copper and brass can survive for fairly long periods, but they too eventually disintegrate.

The metal finds mentioned above were badly corroded and required very special attention using an electrolysis cleaner; but the pot lids, clay tobacco pipe bowls and stoppers were welcome finds. Spare stoppers are always worth keeping because many bottles are found without stoppers and it is convenient to have spares handy. Pot lids and pipe bowls can form entirely separate collections and some enthusiasts devote their entire dump-digging to finding them.

Pot lids were in fact collected in Victorian times, though the hobby was at that time limited to those beautifully coloured specimens found on cosmetics jars. They are now sold in antique shops at several pounds each. Luckily the commoner, everyday lids with transfer designs and lettering were not regarded as worth keeping in the 19th century and they all ended up in rubbish dumps. Being quite solid objects they usually survived the rough treatment all objects receive when they are thrown into dumps and a good fifty per-cent will be found undamaged. Glazes are often crazed but this adds to their charm.

Their history can be traced to the early 19th-century boom in sales of packaged household products. Tooth powders and pastes were among the first to be offered to the public in small jars by chemists who had previously used paper, string and sealing wax. Most chemists of the day made up their own preparations and formulae were closely

6 A brief look at pot lids and clay tobacco pipes

Pot lids

Fig. 24   Pot lids

guarded secrets. This produced an abundance of lids transfer-marked with advertisements claiming that the product in the jar made teeth whiter than anything else on the market, was excellent for the care of the gums, removed nicotine stains and even made a fine mouthwash when mixed with water. The most sought-after specimens are those which could claim royal patronage. One of these was Cherry Tooth Paste, made by John Cosnell & Company of London. The lid bears a superb young Victoria head and the legend, 'Patronized by The Queen.' Another fine example which did not claim royal patronage but which was delightfully designed was 'Woods Areca Nut Tooth Paste'. It sold for sixpence a jar and the advertising blurb on the lid claimed the product was 'For removing tartar and whitening the teeth without damage to the enamel'. The company which manufactured it was based in Plymouth. Many other chemists' preparations were also sold in similar containers.

Meat and fish pastes were soon being offered in pots and jars. 'Burgess's Genuine Anchovy Paste For Toast and Biscuits' bears a royal coat of arms as does 'Fortnum and Mason's Salmon Spread'. Pickles, marmalades, ointments and many other products also produced some excellent specimens. Teas and tobacco were first sold in tin and pewter boxes, but later they too were on sale in jars with delightful lids. In the late 1900s, cosmetics and snuff were also available in the commoner black and white, transfer-marked pots and jars.

78

Dating of pot lids is difficult unless the company whose name appears on the lid can be traced through old newspaper advertisements or if the company is still in business today. A rough guide to dating is provided by the shapes of the lids. The earliest were made to fit tightly into the jar or pot; later a rubber or cork ring was added to provide a better seal; and later still a slot was impressed into the lid to assist removal with the back of a knife blade. Latest of all were those with internal screw threads.

Pot lid repairs

Because they have a fairly high survival rate, pot lids are not normally repaired by collectors. Chipped specimens are usually discarded if the chip has removed part of the transfer. However, I know of one man who specializes in pot lids and I have watched him as work repairing damaged lids. It is very skilful work and requires great patience to reproduce the appearance of lettering and glazes after a hundred years burial; but for those prepared to risk disappointment, here are the basic operations. First, give the lid a thorough wash in a warm water solution of washing-up liquid and ammonia, paying particular attention to the chipped area where tiny spots of grime must be completely removed. Follow this with a second wash in clean water then leave the lid to dry thoroughly.

When absolutely dry, fill the chipped area with fine dental plaster which can be obtained at most chemists' shops. The difficulty lies in matching the off-white or yellowing colour of the old lid; it is done by mixing small amounts of water colour paints with the powder. Allow the repair to dry slowly for at least twenty-four hours before adding the missing areas of the transfer using indian ink and a number of nibs to provide different line widths and designs. After another drying period apply to the lid several coats of clear varnish before giving it a thorough wax polishing. Do not expect immediate success. It can take months of trial and error to achieve an undetectable repair, but the final result can be worth all the effort.

Pipes

Clay tobacco pipes are much easier to repair, which is fortunate because every one you find will have a broken stem. Bowls survive fairly well and they can also be repaired quite easily with a little care and patience if you wish to mend a particularly attractive specimen.

The history of clay tobacco pipes goes back to the introduction of tobacco to England in Tudor times. Deposits of pipe clay, or kaolin, were found in Dorset and there was soon a thriving industry in the West Country where pipes with tiny bowls about half-an-inch in length were manufactured.

By the end of the 17th century, many towns had large, pipe-making factories. Hull, Salisbury, Broseley, Bristol, Chester and London were some of the most important production areas, but there were many small firms in other towns. The pipes were hand-made in a two-piece iron mould which held a plug of wet clay. This was opened out with a conical plunger to form a bowl. The stem was made by rolling wet clay around a steel wire which projected into the bowl.

Early 16th-century stems were only four inches in length, but by the 17th century stems had increased to about eight inches. In the 18th century the 'Alderman', a pipe with a straight stem approximately twelve inches long, was introduced. Later the 'Churchwarden' with a stem two or even three feet long enjoyed a period of popularity. Finally, in the 19th century, the 'Cutty', a pipe with a seven-inch stem, became the generally accepted design.

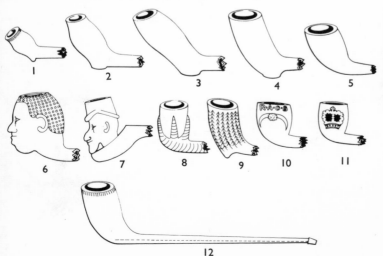

Fig. 25 Types of pipe bowls. 1—16th century; 2—17th century; 3—Alderman; 4 — Churchwarden; 5—19th century; 6-12 — late 19th-century decorations on bowls; 12—repaired stem using 'Sofenbak' and steel wire

Bowls provide a fairly reliable method of dating your finds. Sixteenth-century pipes had tiny, half-inch bowls placed at a steep forward angle to the stem. They often had incised bands around the top of the bowl. By the 17th century, as tobacco became less expensive, bowls had increased in size to twice that of the previous century and a flat foot was added to the base of the bowl so that it could be placed on a table top without scorching the wood.

Eighteenth-century 'Aldermans' and 'Churchwardens' had bowls up to two inches long. They still tended to slope forward from the stem, and it was not until the 19th century that they took on a more rounded shape with the bowl nearer to a right angle with the stem. Marks, particularly initials on the bases of bowls, can date a pipe to within a very limited period. It became a common practice in the late 17th century for makers to initial the bases of the pipes they made. The initials should be read while holding the pipe in the correct smoking position with the bowl to the front. The Christian name initial will then be on the left; the surname on the right. Local archaeological societies have compiled lists of most known makers in their areas together with the periods during which each maker was operating. Reference to these lists will often enable a pipe to be dated by the initials to within a ten- or twenty-year period.

Another method of marking pipes adopted in the 18th and 19th centuries was the rebus—a representation of the maker's name by a figure or a particular design. One example of these early trade marks is seen on the pipes made by the Gauntlett family of Amesbury. Their rebus, usually impressed on the side of the bowl, was a glove or gauntlet. This idea was adopted in the 19th century by masonic orders and by publicans. Pipe bowls bearing buffalo horns or made in the shape of acorns were specially made for lodges of the Royal Ancient Order of the Buffaloes and for the Ancient Order of the Druids. Taverns with names such as *The Grapes* or *The Bull* would have pipes made with bowls shaped as bunches of grapes or bull heads which were given free to customers who purchased their tobacco on the premises. This idea was also copied by tobacconists and by military regiments.

By the late 19th century, special pipe bowls were often made to commemorate famous events or people. A friend of mine found a bowl shaped like a balloon which commemorated a balloon ascent near Vauxhall Bridge in London. Political figures were also immortalized in pipe bowls, and Queen Victoria's head was a common subject with many makers.

Newcomers to pipe-collecting are often surprised at the number of pipe bowls which are found in even quite small dumps. This is because the stems were very fragile and broke easily. A heavy smoker might get through half a dozen pipes in a week. They were also very inexpensive items, selling in the 1850s for as little as a farthing apiece. Many were also given away at taverns and coffee houses. The introduction of cigarettes in the 1870s gradually killed off pipe-making as an important industry, and by 1910 there were only a handful of makers still in existence. This is worth knowing when dating rubbish dumps. Few, if any, broken stems or bowls will be found in dumps made after 1900.

Riversides are probably better collecting areas for clay tobacco pipes than are rubbish dumps if you wish to build up a collection of 16th-, 17th- and 18th-century examples. Best locations are important rivers such as the Thames and Severn and well used harbours or barge moorings.

Pipe repairs

The majority of bowls are found complete with an inch or two of stem remaining. To repair them you need a length of straight wire for each bowl and a packet of 'Sofenbak' modelling compound which is sold at most artists' materials shops. Try repairing a shorter stem before attempting something more difficult like a two-foot 'Churchwarden'. Late 19th-century pipes with decorated bowls require a piece of wire a little over seven inches long. This is pushed into the hole in the remaining portion of the stem and held in place with a plug of plasticine which is placed in the bowl where the wire will be seen to protrude from the stem.

To repair a single pipe with a seven-inch stem place four

heaped tablespoonfulls of Sofenbak into a small dish and add two tablespoonfulls of boiling water. Stir briskly and allow the material to go cold. It should then have the consistency of moist clay. Now it must be formed into a cylinder slightly thicker than the broken end of the pipe stem. I do this by extruding the Sofenbak through a small plastic tube made by cutting two or three inches from the outer case of an empty ballpoint pen. I hold a finger over one end of the tube until I have filled it with the material and then, as more Sofenbak is pushed in, a cylinder-like extrusion comes out at the other end. It is best to extrude the cylinder onto a flat board which can be easily moved around.

Make sure the cylinder is quite straight and set it aside for twenty-four hours. At the end of this period the Sofenbak will have hardened to form a crust on its outer surface strong enough to support its own weight, yet the centre will still be quite soft. This is the time to push the wire attached to the pipe bowl down the centre of the cylinder. Dip your fingers in water and you will be able to re-soften and mould the material around the joint. Allow a further day for hardening and the modelling compound can then be shaped with fairly coarse sandpaper to the rough appearance of the original stem. The mouthpiece can be carefully cut with a modelling knife, leaving a short piece of wire visible at the end, and you should then allow one more day for the Sofenbak to form a thicker crust. On the fourth day you will be able to withdraw the wire with a pair of pliers. Do this with a single, flowing movement and the stem will not break.

Final shaping should be carried out with wet-and-dry carborundum paper sprinkled with a few specks of instant coffee. This will add a realistic colour to the stem which should blend perfectly with the bowl. A further day for hardening will leave you with a repaired pipe almost undetectable from the original.

Bowls can also be repaired with Sofenbak by filling them first with a plug of plasticine and moulding the modelling compound over the damaged area. Sand down after three or four days and the plasticine can then be removed to leave a perfect bowl.

Bottle collecting makes an ideal subject for a group project whatever the size or average age of the group. Single families, a dozen club enthusiasts or an entire class of schoolchildren can all gain a great deal of pleasure from such a project. Properly organized, it holds interest for everyone, can easily be linked to handicraft activities, local history or sociological studies, is flexible enough to cope with outdoor sunshine and the rain which can bring other projects to a standstill and has the added bonus of a fine collection of old bottles for the home, clubhouse or classroom.

The key to the success of a group project is organization; and the first step towards organization is to decide exactly what the project's aims will be. A family might decide to excavate the entire contents of a dump associated with an abandoned and isolated house; a club might attempt to locate every dump used by a village during the past two hundred years; while a large group of children could study the Victorian eating and drinking habits of an entire community.

Having decided on the aims of the project, the necessary work falls into three quite separate activities—research, surveys and actual digging. The various research tasks should be allotted to individuals or to small units. One unit might devote its attention to the local library; another might be assigned the task of interviewing old people in the area, or investigating at the town hall, newspaper offices or museum. At the headquarters of the project, which might be the front room, clubhouse or classroom, a unit must be given the job of correlating the information gathered by the entire team. Large-scale maps of the area might be pinned up on walls, a model of the area could be made or diagrams and plans drawn. All possible site locations collected by each unit should be pinpointed, and those cross-referenced by two or more units marked for particular attention.

Once likely bottle sites have been located in this way and the necessary permission for surveys has been obtained from landowners, it is time for the fieldwork to commence. Teachers and group leaders must ensure that all members involved in field surveys are properly equipped with

Fig. 26 Schoolchildren enjoying a bottle hunt on a riverside

suitable clothing, gloves, and footwear. During initial surveys only one or two members of the group need carry probe rods and digging forks, but all members should carry notepads and pencils to record everything they see or find.

Once actual excavations get under way it is far better, when a large group is involved, to spread the work in such a way that no more than half a dozen members are digging at any particular time. Rarely is it possible to locate a site which will provide a digging face long enough to allow greater numbers to work at the same time. Meanwhile, other members of the group will be engaged on packing finds carefully for transportation to headquarters. Large quantities of old newspaper and a plentiful supply of plastic bags are required for this essential work.

Cleaning should be organized on much the same lines. One unit must be set to cleaning particularly dirty bottles with sand and gravel while the main body is engaged on soaking the bulk of the finds. Other members can arrange drying and polishing work. Cataloguing is easily divided into separate tasks with each unit responsible for identifying and recording different types of bottles and jars. Careful

85

Fig. 27 These children
found a bumper site in a
wood near their home

note-taking should again be encouraged and if more than
one site has been excavated the location of each find must
also be recorded.

If the project is a sociological study the finds might be
catalogued into different types of food and beverage containers. Graphs might be drawn to compare the consump-
tion of different products with the population of the area
during the contemporary period or information about
common ailments in the 19th century might be gained by
studying medicine bottles and their embossing. The history
and popularity of local breweries or favourite drinks might
also be investigated. Members could write to manufacturers of products still on the market to seek advice on
identifying certain products; while others could list the
various types of bottles found—sheared lips, applied lips,

three-piece moulds, and other varieties. The history of glass and of bottle manufacture might make a separate study project, and this is particularly worthwhile if a visit to a modern glassworks can be arranged.

If the bottles are to be used for display or decorative work a wide field is open to teachers and organizers. Vases, lampstands and candlesticks can be made by even the youngest members of the group. Older members could attempt models in bottles or make shelves on which to display the entire collection. Lighting arrangements provide another artistic field as does the making of plaster casts of richly embossed bottles. If there is a keen amateur photographer in the group bottles and jars make excellent subjects for photography. They can also be used as subjects for still-life painting and drawing. A group with a tumbler or other lapidary equipment will be able to use coloured glass for imitation gems. Rings, bracelets and other items of jewellery can be made for a few pence if glass and pottery fragments are used in this way. For older groups, the chemistry of coloured glass would make an interesting

87

Fig. 29 An advanced piece of equipment. This floating suction dredge has been used by the author to recover clay tobacco pipes and small bottles from rivers up to thirty feet deep

project as would comparisons between modern and Victorian packaging and advertising methods.

If the dumps excavated are rich in other finds, such as clay tobacco pipes and pot lids, further possibilities for study and handicrafts are opened up. It might be possible to trace the site of a local pipe factory by initials on pipe bowls; or locate long demolished chemist shops by checking addresses on toothpaste pot lids and other products. Contact with the local archaeological group can also be very rewarding. It might be possible to arrange a talk by a local member; and your group might even be able to help the society by donating rare or unrecorded bottles, clay tobacco pipes and other finds to their collection.

Then there are the possibilities of exchanging bottles with pen-friends or other schools, particularly in the United States, Canada and Australia where the hobby has massive followings. This could lead to a very extensive club or school bottle collection from all over the world.

Finally, there is the book of the project which each member can help in writing and illustrating.

Some readers will be unable to indulge in the physical exertions of dump-digging or, for various reasons, have to limit themselves to digs or underwater searches within the immediate vicinities of their neighbourhood where sites of interest may not turn up. This need not rule out the possibility of owning a fine collection of bottles, jars, pot lids or clay tobacco pipes.

I know many collectors who have fine displays which they have built up by buying unwanted specimens and duplicates from more active enthusiasts. Of course, they miss some of the excitement, but this certainly does not prevent them enjoying the other pleasures of the hobby. There is as much enjoyment in historical research, cleaning, repairing and displaying as there is in actually digging finds out of the ground. Most bottle diggers have duplicates which they sell or barter with other collectors, and you will be able to contact them through The British Bottle Collectors' Club (address given on p. 95) or by advertising in newspapers and magazines. Bottle prices are not too high and so long as you are prepared to limit your collection to commoner varieties, expenditure on a fairly good display need not be more than a few pounds. Pipe and pot lid collectors who are prepared to learn the finer points of repairing these items can always pick up damaged specimens very cheaply.

Bottle diggers interested in the commercial aspects of the hobby will find a ready market for glass marble mineral waters and stone ginger beers at many antique shops; but unless the antique dealer is acquainted with the finer points of bottle collecting, or has customers who are collectors, the prices he offers you for less well-known varieties will be too low. Never sell to such dealers for a price you know to be far less than the specimens are worth; and who better to assess the worth of any bottle than the person who spent days or weeks hunting the site, hours of back-breaking digging to recover it, and a great deal of time and patience on cleaning and polishing it? You will fare much better selling less well-known varieties to other collectors who will readily appreciate the value of your time and effort.

Many bottle dealers started by passing on odd specimens

8 Buying and selling

for small sums to friends and neighbours who admired their collections. This is an excellent method of making a start as a bottle dealer because it requires no outlay on advertising or on any sort of retail premises. Simply invite your friends home to see your collection and you will soon have your first customer.

If you do decide to go in for bottle dealing as a business, you must first ensure a reliable supply of good quality bottles. Do not make the mistake of starting unless you are quite certain you will not run out of stocks. No dump holds an inexhaustible supply of finds, and digging a sufficient number to stock even a small shop or stall takes a great deal of time and effort which could leave you little or no time for actual selling. You will also need a wide variety of bottles if you are to attract plenty of customers and that means a wide variety of dumps, often in different parts of the country. Husband and wife teams, or small groups of diggers, can often succeed with this type of operation because the work of running the retail premises and that of finding the stocks can be shared.

A far better method of acquiring stocks for one-man or one-woman enterprises is to buy some bottles from other diggers to augment your own finds, then add your profit to arrive at the selling price. It is a system which works extremely well if you can keep your suppliers and your customers happy with fair prices. Remember that diggers must add delivery charges if they bring or send bottles to you from distant sites; and do not forget your own over-heads and other expenses which must all be added on, together with your profit, to arrive at the correct selling price.

A good reputation is essential for success in any business venture, and it can be only too easily lost if you treat suppliers or customers unfairly. Never buy or sell poor quality bottles and jars. Avoid cracked and chipped speci-mens and do not sell bottles which have not been thorough-ly cleaned, unless this is understood by the customer who is prepared to buy at a slightly reduced rate and carry out his own cleaning. Make these your golden rules and with a lot of hard work you could end up with a thriving business.

By far the best location for selling bottles is a stall at a regular and well-attended antique market. Rents for stalls are usually very reasonable, and it is often possible to arrange the sharing of a stall with another dealer selling entirely different objects. Remember that bottles look best when well displayed. Set out your stall attractively and you can be sure of many interested callers. Few other dealers at the market will be able to offer such beautiful, decorative, craftsman-made items, often more than one hundred years old, for anything like the prices at which you can sell. Interest potential customers by telling them all you can about the history of any particular item which catches their eye. Improve your knowledge of every aspect of the hobby —bottles, jars, pot lids and pipes—and your enthusiasm is certain to attract newcomers to a hobby which holds as much interest as any enjoying popularity today.

Setting up a stall

City dwellers have a definite advantage when it comes to renting a stall. The larger cities, notably London, have many markets where space can be rented from a few pence to several pounds per day, depending upon the locality, the facilities provided, and the spending power of potential customers.

At the lower end of the scale are the flea markets with small, open platform stalls selling everything from Brussel sprouts to second-hand coats and dresses. Rents are nominal and services Spartan. Do not expect heating or lighting to be laid on and be prepared to put up with 'spivs' and barrow-boys shouting themselves hoarse in order to attract customers. On the other hand, it would be wrong to dismiss all flea markets out of hand. Many are tourist attractions which draw large crowds eager for bargains and unusual souvenirs. You will certainly find no shortage of potential customers, and a well laid-out stall could convert that potential to profitable sales.

Remember that the choice of location is wide. Before renting your stall, spend a few days visiting as many markets as possible. Check on stalls selling anything which falls into the antique or bric-à-brac categories, and spend some time counting the number of customers who buy. Do not make the mistake of asking the stallholder if business is good. He will sense competition and invariably tell you that business is terrible. Keep a careful eye open for tourists and large crowds around particular stalls. If all the business is going to the greengrocers look elsewhere for your chosen site. If the customers are buying old pianos, old books and bric-à-brac the potential for bottle sales is definitely there.

Incidentally, do not neglect flea markets held at unusual times or on odd days. Sunday morning markets are becoming increasingly popular, as are evening markets held during summer months only. One day or evening per week is an excellent method of starting your bottle business; while the really enterprising dealer will have the remainder of the week to devote to a shop or a stall at some other venue.

Markets charging rents of several pounds per day are usually of the covered-in, supermarket type where you will rent what is in fact an open-fronted shop in a neat and orderly row of identical units. Shouting your wares at the customers is definitely frowned upon in such places, where you can be sure of luxuries such as electric lighting and heating. It is probable that the market will be exclusive, that is, devoted entirely to stalls selling a particular variety of goods. Bottles come into the antique category, but you should shop around at a number of such antique markets before deciding on a location. Some specialize in very expensive antique furniture and attract customers expecting to spend several hundred pounds on a single purchase. Avoid such spots and look instead for markets selling smaller and less expensive antiques, particularly porcelain, horse brasses, snuff boxes, coins, medals and similar collectors' items. Once again you will not waste any time spent on checking half a dozen markets to find out more about the number of customers and the items which appear to sell best. Look particularly for empty booths or stalls. If there are large numbers it is a fair indication that the market is not well patronized, either because it is off the beaten track or because the customers are finding better bargains elsewhere.

Country dwellers may find business better if they are prepared to travel to a city market to sell their bottles, although there are many thriving market towns in country districts where a bottle stall could pay excellent dividends. Visit those within ten or twenty miles of your home. An excellent method of checking on the potential for a bottle stall at a country market is to count the number of antique shops in the town. If there are half a dozen such shops, this can be taken as a good indication that there is an antique-orientated buying public in the High Street.

Whatever your final choice—flea market, antique super-market or country town—you must contact the Market Superintendent in order to rent a stall. This official is always present during the early hours when stalls are being set up or booths unlocked. Ask him if there are vacant stalls, find out about rents and the minimum period for which you can rent on a trial basis. If you are offered a stall, take a good look at it or the site it will occupy. It may be in an out-of-the-way corner; it may be too small or too large; or the rent may be far higher than you wish to pay. Never sign a lease until you are absolutely certain that the stall you rent is as near to perfect for your requirements as possible. Remember that the Market Superintendent's job is to ensure that as many stalls as possible are profitably leased. He is as good at selling stall space as you must be at selling bottles. Make your own decision based on your own observations and your own opinion of the market's potential as a site from which to sell bottles.

Notes on pricing

At the time of writing (April 1972) bottle prices in Britain are in a state of flux. On the one hand, an ever-increasing number of less active collectors, who do not involve themselves with bottle recovery, are buying from established dealers. The effect of this increase in collectors is to push prices for top quality bottles ever higher. On the other hand, the number of collectors who dig their own bottles and sell duplicates is increasing by leaps and bounds. These new bottle buffs quite naturally hang on to their best finds and, whenever possible, exchange unwanted bottles with collectors in other parts of the country. Those bottles which do find their way on to the market from this source are more often than not bottles which circulated nationally during the period in which they were in use and which are, therefore, found in many dumps.

Thus, we have rising prices for bottles which had a restricted and localized circulation, such as those issued by small or extinct breweries, mineral water makers and other small companies; while nationally known bottles and jars tend to have static or even falling prices in those areas where the number of bottle diggers is increasing. These market conditions are similar in some ways to those pertaining in the numismatic world. A coin which was minted in vast quantities is usually worth far less than a coin with a low mintage figure. The other deciding factors are condition and demand, both of which apply equally to bottles.

This is a fairly straightforward supply and demand situation, but it is complicated by two factors which do not apply to coins. The first is the insatiable demand for British bottles in the United States, Australia and New Zealand. There are thousands of collectors in these countries prepared to pay excellent prices for commoner British bottles and more and more British dealers are selling overseas, in spite of very high shipping charges.

The other complication is the equally insatiable demand in Britain and overseas for Codd's bottles and stone ginger beers. Glass marble bottles and transfer-marked ginger beers are neither particularly old nor particularly scarce; yet they are prized by people with no interest in other bottles. Retail prices for both have doubled from fifty pence to one pound in less than a year, and there is every indication that they will double again before this year is out. Rarer varieties with particularly rich embossing or unusual colouring fetch far more.

I do not wish to catalogue the prices of bottles in this book because the information will be out of date before the book is published. Check the sales columns of magazines such as *Exchange and Mart*, or *Bottles and Relics* for current price fluctuations, and join the British Bottle Collectors' Club if you want information on which bottles serious collectors are looking for. As a rough guide you can be sure of good demand and prices at least equal to those commanded by Codd's bottles for low circulation beers, quack medicines, Hamiltons and miniature inks. Varieties such as white stoneware, sheared lips, and most unembossed aqua glass do not fetch particularly high prices in Britain, though there is alway good demand from overseas. My final advice to all new dealers is never sell for a low price simply to make a sale. The supply of bottles is not inexhaustible, and many dumps are being lost forever beneath the current building boom.

Useful addresses

Britain:
> British Bottle Collectors' Club,
> The Secretary,
> 49 Elizabeth Road,
> Brentwood, Essex.

U.S.A.:
> 'Bottles and Relics',
> 110 West Elizabeth,
> Austin, Texas, 78704.

Australia:
> Australian Bottle Collectors' Club,
> Secretary,
> 39 Ellington Street,
> Ekibin,
> Queensland, 4121.

Suppliers of bottle cutters:
> A.A.B. Developments Ltd.,
> 236a North End Road,
> London, W.14.

Suppliers of 'Sofenbak':
> Windsor & Newton Ltd.,
> Wealdstone,
> Harrow, Middlesex.

Index (Plate numbers refer to the coloured illustrations)